Sarasota's

CHEF
DU JOUR

Sarasota's # CHEF DU JOUR

*Favorite Chef Recipes
from Sarasota's
most popular
restaurants*

By
Jan McCann

STRAWBERRY PRESS, SARASOTA, FLORIDA

PHOTO CREDITS
Sarastoa Historical Archives - *Mary Jane Whitaker*
Historic Spanish Point - *Mrs. Palmer Potter*
John and Mable Ringling Museum of Art - *Ringling Museum*
Selby Botanical Gardens - *Marie Selby*
Rebecca Wild Baxter - *Gulf to Bay*
Iris Rosenberg - *The Fish Market*

COVER & BOOK DESIGN:
Nora A. Hooper

RECIPE ILLUSTRATIONS:
Nora A. Hooper

1ST PRINTING 1992, 1,000 COPIES
2ND PRINTING 1993, 2,000 COPIES
3RD PRINTING 1994, 3,000 COPIES
4TH PRINTING 1995, 3,000 COPIES

ISBN 0-9640198-4-1

Strawberry Press, 3712 Woodmont Dr., Sarasota, FL 34232

To my husband Kim, who supported me throughout this endeavor. To my daughter, Karen who helped immensely with the typing. To Cindy and Roland Long, my best friends. To my parents who have always shown me the way.

Acknowledgement

To all the great chefs and all the good food in Sarasota.
It's the everyday achievements of these chefs that make
Sarasota exquisite to visit or a pleasure to stay a lifetime.

Alexanders	L'Auberge du Bon Vivant
Augie's Front Burner	Le Petit Jardin Cafe
Banyan Restaurant	Limerick Junction
Beach Bistro	Main Bar
Beach Cafe and Bar	Marina Jack
Beasley's	Marina Jack II
Bella Roma	Melting Pot
Bellinis	Michael's On East
Bijou Cafe	Milano's
Brass Parrot	Millies
Bridge Tender Inn	Miramar
Cafe Baci	Mr. Hors d'Oeuvre
Cafe L'Europe	Nellie's Deli
Cafe Vienna	Neptune's
Caragiulos	Nick's On the Water
Charley's Crab	Old Heidelberg Castle
Chart House	O'Leary's
Chef Caldwell	Ophelia's
Chez Sylvie	Osteria
Ciao!	Pasta Del Giorno
Coasters	Pastel's
The Colony	Patricks
Columbia	Pelican Alley
Crow's Nest	Piccolo Mondo
Emphasis	Poki Joe's
Euphemia Haye	Poseidon
Ferretti's	Rick's Cafe
Flying Bridge	Roessler's
Gecko's	Sandbar
Harry's Continental	Sarasota Brewing Co.
Hillview Grill	Serving Spoon
Hyatt	Shells
Inner Circle	Summerhouse
Insomniacs	Tudor Rose
Jack's Chophouse Grill	Turtles
Just Desserts	Wildflower

A special thank you to the following restaurants whom we fondly remember.

The Field's, Buccaneer Inn
Casa Amigos
Club Bandstand
Coley's
Maas Brothers
Monique's Artist Palette Cafe
Oasis
Old South Oyster Bar
Peppers
Robin and Joel's
Shenkel's
Stickney Point Fishery
Tassoti's
Vito's
Whisper Inn

Table of Contents

Introduction

This cookbook is a representation of 72 of Sarasota's best restaurants and local fare. The variation is delightful and reflective of Sarasota's diverse ethnic and tropical background. Our Gulf Coast location is rich in seafood and produce. **Chef du Jour** provides creative new ways to prepare local harvests. Each recipe will give you a glimpse of the Chef's unique style and tastes.

Serve up a creation from any of the Chef recipes within and you will be the Chef du Jour!

The Whittaker Homestead.

◆ *Chapter One* ◆

Appetizers
And
Accompaniments

MARY JANE WHITAKER
AT YELLOW BLUFFS

 Born Mary Jane Wyatt on April 11, 1831, she lived a pioneer's life for 77 years, displaying a spirit of courage and resourcefulness.

Being one of the first settlers to the area, William Whitaker chose a high point called Yellow Bluffs. This area is just north of the Centennial park on the bayfront.

William and Mary built a log home and she soon bore their first child, Nancy.

The Whitakers left their home for the protection offered at Branch Fort on the Manatee River. Indian relations had broken down and the Seminoles were beginning to raid area homes. While in the Fort, the Whitakers' first son, Furman, was born.

Upon return to Yellow Bluffs, the Whitakers found their home burned. They rebuilt the wood frame house pictured on the preceding page. The house was completed in 1857 at the corner of North Trail and 12th street.

Four years later the Civil War broke out. Shoes and clothes had to be repaired and made to last. Coffee was made from parched or roasted corn which was grown in the garden. Union blockade gunboats came into Sarasota Bay and the soldiers went ashore to Yellow Bluffs for food and water.

To preserve her own supplies, Mary Jane would chase the chickens and cows into the woods. Union soldiers would find only drinking water and oranges if any were ripe.

In one instance, a Union soldier threatened to burn Mary Jane's house. She called the soldier's bluff, handing him the matches and daring him to burn the house of a defenseless woman. Mary Jane's bravery so impressed the soldier he declined.

Mary Jane Whittaker

When the war ended, Mary Jane focused on educating her large family. Eight children grew to adulthood; two girls having died before maturity. A tutor from Ohio assisted in teaching the three "R"s with Mary Jane providing art lessons.

The children began to leave home and marry. Furman finished medical school and returned to practice in the area. William died in 1888. Mary Jane joined her husband in 1908 in the Pioneer Whitaker Cemetery.

THE SERVING SPOON
1825 South Osprey Ave.

WHOLE WHEAT APPLESAUCE PANCAKES
James Palermo

Makes 20 4" pancakes

2	eggs
1½	cup whole wheat flour
½	cup all purpose flour
1	cup buttermilk
1	cup applesauce
½	tsp. cinnamon
½	Tbs. ground ginger
2	Tbs. honey
2	tsp. baking powder
½	tsp. baking soda
½	stick (4 Tbs.) melted butter

◆ Beat eggs, add rest of wet ingredients (buttermilk, applesauce, honey).
◆ Combine dry ingredients (flours, cinnamon, ginger, baking soda, baking powder).
◆ Add to wet mixture.
◆ Add melted butter and refrigerate*.
◆ Cook on buttered griddle until bubbles form and then flip. Cook until brown.

Serve hot!

Extras: Before flipping, add fresh apple slices covered with cinnamon sugar or fresh bananas.

•James recommends making the batter the day before you plan to serve them. This will insure a better rise.

Limerick Junction Pub and Club

1296 First Street, Sarasota

Irish Beer Bread
Michael Gordan

Makes one loaf

First buy a 6 pack of Guinness Stout. Drink two!

2	*cups self rising flour*
3	*Tbs. sugar*
3	*Tbs. butter*
12	*oz. Guinness*
1	*egg*
½	*tsp. baking soda*

Preheat oven to 350°

Note: *Beer must be room temperature.*

- ◆ Sift flour, sugar, and soda.
- ◆ Mix beer, egg, and melted butter.
- ◆ Mix with dry ingredients.
- ◆ Grease loaf pan.
- ◆ Bake 15 minutes, turn pan and bake 15 minutes more.
- ◆ Check with a toothpick.

FERRETTI'S
5767 Beneva Rd., Sarasota

BAGNA CAUDA
Chef Rich Ferretti

Serves 6-10
Dipping sauce:
- ½ cup butter (¼ lb.)
- ½ cup olive oil
- 6 cloves garlic, minced
- 2 cans 4 oz. anchovies
- ¼ cup cream, optional

Fresh vegetables: trim and cut
- cauliflower
- carrots
- bell peppers
- celery
- celery cabbage, (bok choy)
- garlic bread

◆ Chop anchovies, mince garlic fine, or put in a blender with 1/4 cup olive oil to mince.

◆ Saute in pan until bubbling. Add butter and heat slowly for 2-3 minutes.

◆ Add cream if you desire.

◆ Serve warm as a dip for vegetables or, in individual servings with vegetables and garlic bread.

Marina Jack
2 Marina Plaza, Sarasota

Pico de Gallo
Mary Moreno

Makes 2 cups

1	small bunch cilantro
1	half fresh lime
1	medium sweet white onion
1	medium red onion
1	bunch scallions
⅛	cup minced garlic
¼	cup green chilies, chopped (fresh or canned will work)
1	large cucumber
2	large tomatoes
1	medium jalapeno
	Salt and pepper to taste
½	cup red wine vinegar
⅛	cup sugar

◆ Finely chop cilantro. Peel and seed cucumber and cut to a small dice. Seed and mince jalapeno. Finely dice all onions and tomatoes.

◆ Put all the above ingredients in a large bowl. Add salt, pepper, garlic, sugar, and chilies. Pour in vinegar and squeeze in lime juice.

◆ Chill for at least half an hour to allow the flavors to marry.

◆ Can be served with blackened fish, chicken, quesadillas, or chips. This salsa will keep several days in the refrigerator.

Nellie's Deli and Market
3688 Webber Street, Sarasota

Nellie's Chopped Liver
Serves 6 as an appetizer or 12 as a spread

2	*large Spanish onions*
1½	*lbs. chicken livers*
9	*eggs, hard-boiled*
	salt*
	black pepper*
	granulated garlic*

- ◆ Saute coarsely chopped onions until golden brown. Drain and remove.
- ◆ In same pan, saute chicken livers until thoroughly cooked. Drain and remove. Let cool.
- ◆ You can put through meat grinder on coarse, or chop the onions, livers, and eggs.
- ◆ *Mix and taste for seasonings.
- ◆ Serve cold with crackers as a spread or on lettuce as an appetizer.

Main Bar
1944 Main Street, Sarasota

Hummus
Family Recipe

Makes 1 Quart

4	cups garbanzo beans, drained, cooked reserve liquid
½	cup lemon juice, or to taste
3	Tbs. sesame seed paste (Tahini)
2	Tbs. garlic, granulated or fresh
½	tsp. salt, or to taste

◆ Blend in food processor of blender, adding bean juice as needed for semi-thick but smooth consistency.

◆ Serve on platter.

◆ Make a well in the center to put olive oil in. Surround with pita bread cut into quarters.

Optional: sprinkle with paprika, cumin, crushed red pepper flakes, or minced parsley.

Better to be alone than in bad company.

Anonymous

NELLIE'S DELI AND MARKET
3688 Webber Street, Sarasota

BASIL PESTO
Jim Jones

Makes 2 cups

Puree in food processor or blender, combine:
- 2 *cups basil leaves, fresh, thoroughly washed and patted dry*
- 1 *cup Pignoli (pine nuts) nuts*
- 4 *large garlic cloves, chopped*
  - *olive oil to thin*

When you have this thoroughly blended and to the right consistency, add:
- 1 *cup Parmesan cheese, grated*
- ¼ *cup Romano cheese, grated*
  - *salt and black pepper to taste*

Mix in with your favorite pasta, fluff into hot rice or stir into homemade mayonnaise as a sauce for cold poached fish or vegetables.

THE BRIDGE TENDER INN
135 Bridge Street, Bradenton Beach

GRILLED PORTOBELLO MUSHROOM
Kathy Eubanks

1 per person

1	lg. Portobello mushroom
4	oz. pasta, linguini, or angel hair
6	oz. garlic butter
¼	cup Italian salad dressing
3	Tbs. olive oil
½	cup basil, fresh
	Parmesan cheese, freshly grated

◆ Remove stem from mushroom.

◆ Mix Italian dressing, olive oil, and fresh basil together and marinate mushroom and stem for at least two hours. This can be done a day ahead.

◆ Cook pasta.

◆ Grill mushroom for three minutes on each side.

◆ Mix pasta and 3 oz. garlic butter together and sprinkle with Parmesan cheese.

◆ Place mushroom and stem on top of pasta and finish with a dollop of garlic butter.

◆ This is an impressive appetizer.

BEASLEY'S
277 South Gate Shopping Plaza, Sarasota

CRAB STUFFED MUSHROOMS
Jon Sutter

Makes 4 servings

8	large mushroom caps
½	lb. crab meat
¼	cup celery, chopped fine
2	Tbs. onion, chopped fine
1	tsp. garlic powder
½	tsp. oregano
1	Tbs. parsley flakes
1	tsp. white pepper
½	cup bread crumbs
¼	lb. butter, melted

◆ Wash the mushroom caps, dry, and set aside.
◆ Mix all of the ingredients together.
◆ Stuff each mushroom cap with the mixture.
◆ Spoon some of the melted butter over top of each mushroom.
◆ Cook at 350° for 10 minutes.
◆ Garnish each cap with parsley flakes.
◆ Serve with a lemon wedge.

Whatever is in the heart will come up to the tongue.
Persian Proverb

THE COLONY BEACH AND TENNIS RESORT

1620 Gulf of Mexico Drive, Longboat Key

STONECRAB CAKE
Chef Jean-Pierre Pellet

Serves 4

- 1 *lb. stonecrab meat*
- ½ *lb. mixed nuts (pistachio, almonds and hazelnuts)*
- 1 *lb. spinach, fresh*
- 1 *roasted red bell pepper (available in can from gourmet grocery store)*
- 1½ *cups bread crumbs*

For breading:
- 5 *eggs, beaten*
- *flour*
- 1 *cup pecans, finely chopped*

♦ Into mixing bowl, place crab meat. Combine with mixed nuts, chopped pimentos (finely diced), spinach (blanched and chopped), mayonnaise, cayenne pepper, hot mustard, and bread crumbs.

♦ Mix well with spatula. Place mixture about 1/2" thick into molds.

♦ Place in freezer until just a little firm - not frozen through.

♦ Remove from molds. Dip each cake in egg, then in mixture of pecans and flour. Cover cake completely with breading.

♦ Saute in clarified butter and a little oil in a frying pan.

♦ Serve with a hot, spicy mayonnaise and/or cocktail sauce.

♦ Makes about eight 6 oz. cakes.
Reduce the amount in molds for more cakes.

Mr. Hors D'Oeuvre
2732 Stickney Point Rd., Sarasota

Marinated Chicken Breast Skewers
Chef Albert Rocuant

Makes 20 Skewers

> 1 lb. chicken breast, large dice
> ½ cup Teriyaki sauce
> ½ cup apple cider
> 1 tsp. oregano
> 3 tsp. garlic, minced
>   salt and pepper to taste

- ◆ Mix ingredients and marinate chicken for 2 hours.
- ◆ Skewer chicken pieces with onion and green pepper chunks on 4 inch bamboo skewers.
- ◆ Bake at 350° for 10 minutes.

This is one of Mr. Hors D'Oeuvres's most popular items!

The Melting Pot
1055 South Tamiami Trail, Sarasota

Fiesta Cheese Fondue
John Robertson

	flour to dredge
8	*oz. beer*
¼	*tsp. garlic, minced*
½	*tsp. Worcestershire*
¼	*tsp. ground mustard*
½	*oz. jalapenos, chopped*
½	*oz. onions, chopped*
2-3	*oz. Picante sauce*
1 2	*oz. sharp cheddar cheese, grated*
4	*oz. Swiss Emmanthaler, grated*

- ◆ Grate the cheese.
- ◆ Combine cheese in a plastic bag and toss with flour until lightly coated.
- ◆ Heat beer in double boiler and stir in spices.
- ◆ Add cheese slowly, stirring constantly.
- ◆ When all cheese has melted whip with a whisk to a fluffy consistency.
- ◆ Fold in Picante sauce and jalepeno.
- ◆ Serve with vegetables, apples, bread, and tortilla chips.

PELICAN ALLEY
1009 West Albee Rd., Nokomis

OYSTERS ROCKEFELLER
Chef Michael Drumgool

Makes 3/4 gallon of sauce

For sauce:
- ½   *medium Spanish onion, chopped*
- 2   *Tbs., chopped garlic*
- 4   *oz. Pernod (liquor)*
- 2   *oz. dry white wine*
- ½   *tsp. crushed black pepper*
- 2   *Tbs. chicken base*
- ½   *cup roux (equal amounts of butter and flour)*
- 1   *qt. heavy cream*
- 3   *lb. frozen chopped spinach, thawed. Press all water out of spinach*

Other ingredients:
shucked oysters   cooked bacon
Parmesan cheese   lemon wedges

- ◆ In a medium pot, saute the onions with the garlic in the Pernod and wine.
- ◆ Add the black pepper, chicken base, and roux. Cook another minute or two then add cream, stirring constantly.
- ◆ Heat the sauce until it has a smooth, thick consistency.
- ◆ Remove from heat and thoroughly blend in the *drained* spinach.
- ◆ Shuck oysters and rinse well. Do not cut bottom muscle, leave attached.

- Top oysters with sauce. Cover the oysters well - place a small piece of cooked bacon on top and sprinkle with Parmesan cheese.
- Place on a cookie sheet and place in preheated 350° - 400° oven.
- Bake for 10-15 minutes, until top is golden but bacon is not overcooked.
- Serve with lemon wedges and enjoy!!

Marie Selby with Wiggles.

◆ *Chapter Two* ◆

Soups, Salads
and Pasta

William and Marie Selby .

MARIE SELBY

 Marie Selby, a quiet woman who enjoyed wearing blue jeans and cowboy boots more than an evening gown, left an enduring imprint on Sarasota.

Born August 9, 1885 in West Virginia, Marie moved with her family to Ohio where she met and married her high school sweetheart, Bill Selby, a wealthy partner in his father's Oil and Gas Company.

In 1909, soon after they were married, the couple took an adventurous cross-country journey by car. They were inspired to attempt such a feat when they heard of America's first cross-continental automobile race from new York City to Seattle. Although not contestants, Marie and Bill traveled the same course. Starting on June 1, 1909, they reached Seattle on June 22, 1909. Bill and Marie took six days less than the winners. That experience qualified Marie as the first woman to cross the United States by auto.

In the early 1920's, the Selbys bought seven acres on Sarasota Bay where they built a modest stucco home among the banyan and laurel trees .

They also owned a 3,000 acre ranch east of Sarasota. Marie was an avid horsewoman, William a rugged outdoorsman who loved to hunt and fish. If not riding or fishing, Marie loved gardening.

The Selbys had no children. After William's death in 1956, the Selby Foundation was established. Today it awards more than $30 million in scholarships and grants to area students, colleges, hospitals, libraries, and programs that enhance our quality of life.

Marie Selby left her home and property and $2 million to establish the Marie Selby Botanical Gardens. She died in 1971. Since then, the Gardens have become a world renowned center for research and education. The Marie Selby Botanical Gardens now include more than 20,000 greenhouse plants and a stunning tropical orchid collection.

The gardens are open to the public for a small admission fee.

CHARLEY'S CRAB
St. Armands Circle, Sarasota

CHILLED RASPBERRY CHAMPAGNE SOUP
Chef Wesley Duval

Serves 6-8

1	qt. frozen raspberries, thawed
6	oz. fresh orange juice
8	oz. heavy cream
8	oz. champagne

- ◆ Combine raspberries, juice, and cream in a large bowl.
- ◆ Mix well.
- ◆ Stir in champagne.
- ◆ Chill and serve in chilled bowls with unsweetened whipped cream and fresh mint.

Soups, Salads & Pasta

THE SURFRIDER
6400 Midnight Pass Road, Siesta Key

CHILLED SMOKY CUCUMBER SOUP WITH SPICY SHRIMP
Javier Arana

Serves 4

Soup Ingredients:
4	tsp. oil
½	lb. potatoes, peeled and diced
¼	cup onions, chopped
¼	cup celery, chopped
1	clove garlic, minced
½	tsp. salt
½	tsp. white pepper
3	cups chicken stock
3	cucumbers, peeled, seeded, and chopped
4	Tbs. barbecue sauce
1	cup heavy cream

◆ Saute onions, celery and garlic in the oil until soft.
◆ Add the stock and bring to a boil. Add potatoes, salt and pepper. Cook until potatoes are tender. Add cucumbers and simmer for five minutes.
◆ Cool. Blend until smooth. Add barbecue sauce and cream. Refrigerate overnight to blend flavors.
◆ To serve, top with spicy shrimp.

Spicy Shrimp ingredients:
12	large shrimp, peeled, deveined with tails on
4	Tbs. olive oil
1	Tbs. whole white peppercorns, cracked
1	Tbs. whole coriander seeds, cracked
½	tsp. coarse salt

◆ Toss shrimp in oil and coat with seasonings. Place on sheet pan. Bake at 450° - 2 minutes. Let cool and serve.

THE BIJOU CAFE
1287 First Street, Sarasota

CREAMY GAZPACHO SOUP
Serves 6-8

4	very ripe tomatoes, peeled and seeded
½	can tomato puree
1	cucumber, peeled and seeded
1	red pepper
1	green pepper
1	small white onion
1	carrot
2	small cans V-8 juice or tomato juice
1	Tbs. virgin olive oil
1	Tbs. fresh garlic, chopped, pinch of oregano, basil and thyme
	salt and pepper to taste
	dash of white Worcestershire sauce, dash of Tabasco sauce
½	cup mayonnaise
½	cup sour cream

◆ Mix mayonnaise and sour cream together and refrigerate.

◆ Place all ingredients except the V-8 juice in a food processor and pulse to get a chunky, **NOT** pureed texture.

◆ Slowly add the V-8 juice until texture is to your liking.

◆ Chill thoroughly, preferably overnight, but at least 4 hours.

◆ Just before serving, blend the sour cream mixture into the Gazpacho with a wire whisk.

◆ If you prefer, you may also serve the sour cream mixture on the side and let guests add it to their own taste.

◆ Serve with fresh hot garlic bread.

EMPHASIS
1301 First Street, Sarasota

ROASTED TOMATO BISQUE

Serves 6

2 lbs. Roma tomatoes halved
2 Tbs. salt
½ cup extra virgin olive oil
1 tsp. crushed red pepper
1 Tbs. dry basil
2 Tbs. crushed garlic
1 small onion - minced

3 cups chicken stock
2 cups heavy cream

◆ Combine first 7 ingredients and marinate for 3 hours at room temperature.

◆ Then cook tomato mixture in slow (200°) oven for 1 hour.

◆ Puree in food processor until smooth.

◆ Add puree to remaining ingredients in large sauce pan and simmer for 30 minutes.

◆ Garnish with chopped fresh basil.

Soups, Salads & Pasta

RICK'S CAFE
8197 South Tamiami Trail, Sarasota

ROASTED PEPPER SOUP
WITH SHRIMP AND BASIL
Rick Rubin

Serves 8

    5   yellow peppers
    5   red peppers
    5   cups chicken broth
        sugar, salt, and crushed red pepper to taste
    1   pint heavy cream
   16   medium fresh shrimp
        fresh basil for garnish
    2   Tbs. cornstarch

◆ Roast peppers on grill until skin is blackened. Put into plastic bag and allow to cool.

◆ When peppers are cool enough to handle, remove from plastic bag and skin should peel off easily.

◆ Remove seeds.

◆ Puree peppers with chicken stock in food processor until very soupy.

◆ Put puree into sauce pan and heat over medium heat. Be careful not to burn bottom.

◆ Add sugar, salt, and crushed red pepper to taste.

◆ Add cream

◆ Mix 2 Tbs. water with 2 Tbs. cornstarch.

◆ Bring soup to a very light boil and add cornstarch mixture to provide a little body.

◆ Chop cooked shrimp into bite size pieces and sprinkle on top of each serving.

◆ Garnish with basil for color.

BELLINIS RISTORANT
1549 Main Street, Sarasota

CREMA DI BROCCOLI *(Cream of Broccoli Soup)*

Serves 4

1	bunch broccoli
1	large onion
¼	lb. butter
	pinch of salt and pepper
1	cup whipping cream
½	cup chicken broth

- ◆ Boil broccoli and onion al dente.
- ◆ Drain, divide in half. Then put in blender with half the whipping cream, salt, pepper and ¼ cup of chicken broth. Actually, you are making two batches because a normal blender will not hold the full amount.
- ◆ Melt butter in sauce pan and add the blended broccoli mixture to it.
- ◆ Reheat but do not boil.
- ◆ Serve when hot.
- ◆ Don't put all the broccoli in blender if you like some crunch in your soup.
- ◆ Top with cheese and croutons.

Soups, Salads & Pasta

Beach Cafe and Bar
431 Beach road, Siesta Key

Broccoli Watercress Cheddar Cheese Soup
Manolo Cancho

Serves 6-8

½	head broccoli
1	bunch watercress, stems removed
5	cups chicken stock
5	Tbs. butter
4	Tbs. flour
1	cup milk
2	cups heavy cream
1	lb. cheddar cheese
	salt and pepper
¼	cup sherry

◆ Peel the stems of the broccoli and chop coarsely.

◆ Break top into 1 inch long flowerets.

◆ Place broccoli and watercress in soup pot with 3 cups of the chicken stock.

◆ Bring to a boil, lower heat and simmer for 5 minutes.

◆ Melt butter over medium heat in a small sauce pan. Stir in flour and cook for 2 minutes, stirring constantly and taking caution not to brown.

◆ Gradually add milk and cream and bring to a gentle boil.

◆ Lower heat and simmer for 5 minutes.

◆ Add cream sauce to broccoli, add remaining 2 cups chicken stock and bring to a boil, lower heat.

◆ Add cheddar cheese and stir occasionally as the cheese melts.

◆ Add salt and pepper to taste and ¼ cup sherry.

◆ Serve hot.

Soups, Salads & Pasta

CROWS NEST RESTAURANT AND TAVERN

1968 Tarpon Center Drive, Venice

DUCHESS SOUP
Owner Steve Harner/Chef Jeff Minkwic

Serves 12

1	cup chopped carrots
1	cup chopped celery
¼	cup chopped onion
⅓	lb. butter
12	oz. flour
⅓	gal. milk
⅓	gal. water
1½	oz. chicken bouillon
1¾	lb. high quality American cheese
1¾	lb. cooked, diced potatoes

- ◆ Simmer carrots and celery in water until tender.
- ◆ Saute onions in butter until translucent.
- ◆ Add flour to form a roux — cook 5 minutes, stirring constantly.
- ◆ At same time heat milk, water and chicken bouillon until near boil, whip in roux until thick.
- ◆ Add cheese and potatoes. Adjust for thickness.

*This is a signature soup of the **Crows Nest** and I thank them very much for sharing it with us!*

Soups, Salads & Pasta

THE BIJOU CAFE
1287 First Street, Sarasota

WHITE BEAN AND SAUSAGE SOUP
Jean Pierre Knaggs

Serves 6-8

1	cup chopped onion
½	cup chopped carrot
½	cup chopped celery
1	Tbs. chopped fresh garlic
1	tsp. thyme
½	Tbs. nutmeg or allspice
2 or 3	bay leaves
1	Tbs. tomato paste
½	lb. bacon (thick cut) diced
2	cups white beans (great northern) soak overnight
5-6	cups homemade chicken stock
½-¾	lb. smoked sausage (kielbasa, etc.)

Optional: *Hot sauce, dry sherry, salt and pepper*

◆ Saute bacon until lightly browned. Remove bacon and set aside.

◆ Saute onions, carrots, and celery in bacon drippings until soft but not browned.

◆ Add garlic and again do not let brown.

◆ Place sauteed vegetables in soup pot with thyme, nutmeg, bay leaves, tomato paste and bacon.

◆ Add chicken stock and drained beans.

◆ Cook at least one hour or until beans are very soft and the soup has thickened somewhat.

◆ Add more chicken stock or water if the soup gets too thick.

- Cut sausage into ½" cubes and saute briefly to remove excess fat.
- Drain sausage on paper towels and add sausage to soup.
- Simmer gently for twenty minutes, season to taste with salt and black pepper.
- Add a few drops of hot sauce if you like it spicy.
- Add a touch of dry (not sweet) sherry just before serving.
- Serve this soup in hand made crocks with lots of warm crusty French bread in front of a roaring fire!

Soups, Salads & Pasta

CAFE VIENNA
2615 Mall Drive, Sarasota

CABBAGE SOUP
Chef Henry Kubala

Serves 12-16

2	onions
2	carrots
8	oz. margarine
½	cup sweet paprika
½	tsp. ground caraway seeds
1	cup crushed tomatoes
1	head green cabbage
½	cup white vinegar
2	Tbs. sugar
	beef stock or bouillon
2	bay leaves
2	large potatoes, peeled and cubed
½	lb. kielbasa, cut in half lengthwise and sliced thin
6	cloves of garlic, pressed
	marjoram
	salt and pepper
	sour cream and fresh chopped parsley for garnish

◆ Chop onions, shred carrots and mix together in large saucepan.

◆ Saute with margarine until fragrant. Mix paprika and caraway in quickly so as not to burn. Put a little water in to help mix.

◆ Add crushed tomato, cabbage (chopped fine), bay leaves, vinegar, sugar, beef stock and salt and pepper to taste. Let simmer for 20 minutes.

◆ Add the cubed potatoes and thinly sliced kielbasa. If you like a spicy flavor, add hot pepper or cayenne pepper to your taste.

- ◆ Cook until potatoes are tender.
- ◆ Just before serving add pressed garlic and marjoram.
- ◆ If you like a thicker consistency you may also add a roux at this time.
- ◆ Ladle soup into serving bowl.
- ◆ Place a dollop of sour cream in the center of each bowl and sprinkle with chopped parsley.

Goten Appetite!

A man shows his character by what he laughs at.

German Proverb

HILLVIEW GRILL
1920 Hillview Street, Sarasota

BLACK-EYE PEAS
Mindy and Miles Millwee

Makes 1 Gallon

2½	lbs. black-eye peas
1½	cups diced celery
1½	cups diced pepper (red or green)
2½	cups diced onion
1½	cups diced carrots
2	cups corn
1	gal. chicken or pork stock (approx.)
1	Tbs. ground black pepper
¼	cup ground coriander
⅛	cup ground cumin
	salt to taste
½	cup vegetable oil

◆ Cover peas with water and bring to a boil.

◆ As water boils away replace liquid with stock.

◆ Continue this process until peas are fully cooked. Remove from heat and set aside.

◆ In a 2 gallon pan heat oil and saute onion, celery, pepper, and carrots until tender.

◆ Stir in salt, pepper, coriander, and cumin. Simmer about 10 minutes.

◆ Add cooked peas to the vegetable mixture.

◆ Bring to a low boil and add corn.

◆ Simmer 15 minutes.

◆ Correct the seasonings and serve.

CHEZ SYLVIE
1526 Main Street, Sarasota

CARROT SOUP
Owner Sylvie Routier

2	lb. carrots
½	large onion
2	qt. chicken Veloute:
2½	oz. butter
⅓	cup flour
2	qt. chicken stock
1	tsp. sugar depending on the sweetness of the carrots
	Half and half or cream
½	Tbs. fresh dill
	salt and white pepper

- ◆ Cut up peeled carrots and onion into uniform slices.
- ◆ Cover with chicken stock and simmer until carrots are tender.
- ◆ Puree carrots and onion, reserve.
- ◆ To make veloute: Cook butter and flour over medium heat stirring (so not to brown flour) for 10 minutes. Let cool, then add hot but not boiling, chicken stock. Stir with whip until roux is dissolved, bring to a boil stirring constantly. Reduce heat and simmer 20 minutes.
- ◆ Add carrot puree and cream to veloute.
- ◆ Season with dill, salt, pepper, and sugar to taste.

WILDFLOWER NATURAL FOOD RESTAURANT

5218 Ocean Blvd., Siesta Key

CARROT (BUNNY LOVE) SOUP
Chef Marc Henri

Serves 4

1	lb. carrots, organic
1	rib celery
1	small onion
2	cloves garlic
2	bay leaves
1	Tbs. thyme
8	oz. extra firm tofu
½	cup cashew pieces
	honey
	Vegi Sal* (vegetable salt seasoning)
	fresh dill

- Peel carrots and cut onions, celery, and carrots into pieces.
- Place in soup pot and cover with water (2 inches above the vegetables).
- Add bay leaves, thyme, garlic.
- Bring to a boil, reduce heat, cover and simmer until the carrots are soft. Remove the bay leaves.
- Puree in batches in food processor or blender.
- With last batch add the tofu, and cashew, and puree until smooth with no remaining lumps. Add this to the soup.
- Season with Vegi Sal.
- Add honey to taste (the sweeter the carrots the less you'll need). Garnish with fresh chopped dill and enjoy!

*Vegi Sal is available at The Granary.

Soups, Salads & Pasta

MIRAMAR AT THE QUAY
216 Sarasota Quay, Sarasota

BLACK BEAN SOUP
Nicolas Maisonett

Serves 4

1	lb. dry black beans
2	medium onions, small dice
1	medium green pepper, small dice
¼	cup fresh chopped garlic
2	heaping tsp. cumin
1	cup olive oil
1½	tsp. sugar
3	bay leaves
1½	tsp. white pepper
2	tsp. salt
2	qt. water (enough to cover beans plus 2 inches of water)

◆ Wash beans with cold water. Place beans in a sauce pan with the 2 quarts of water. Bring to a boil, remove from heat and cover.

◆ In a frying pan at medium heat, add olive oil. When hot add chopped garlic.

◆ Saute until golden brown and add chopped onions and green pepper.

◆ Add all the spices except for salt and sugar.

◆ Saute this mixture for about 10 minutes and add to sauce pan with beans. At this point, add the salt, sugar, and cover.

◆ Let this cook at medium heat for about an hour or until beans are tender.

◆ Serve over a bed of white rice with chopped raw onions.

Soups, Salads & Pasta

O'LEARY'S
Island Park - Bayfront, Sarasota

CAPTAIN BILL'S CAJUN CHICKEN SOUP
Serves 4-6

2-2½	lb. chickens
1	green pepper, chopped
1	red bell pepper, chopped
1	cup chopped celery
½	cup chopped onion
½	cup chopped scallions
3	cloves garlic
	coarse ground black pepper
	cayenne pepper
	red pepper and salt
1	qt. Sauterne wine

- Boil chicken in water until meat flakes easily from bone. Set aside until cool enough to remove bones and skin. Save broth.
- Chop chicken into 1 inch pieces.
- In a large pot or Dutch oven, saute onions, scallions, and garlic in 2-3 Tbs. of oil.
- Add all other ingredients including salt and pepper to taste.
- Pour in 1 qt. wine.
- Add chicken pieces.
- Pour in sufficient broth to obtain desired consistency.
- Cover and simmer for 1 hour
- Serve as is, or over cooked rice.

Piccolo Mondo Ristorante
3131 Clark Road, Sarasota

Stracciatella In Brado
Chef Carlo Tonelli

Serves 8

12	cups chicken broth
5	eggs
4	cups freshly grated parmesan cheese
1	cup bread crumbs
4	tsp. freshly grated nutmeg
2	tsp. fresh lemon juice
1	tsp. grated black pepper

- In a large pot, bring chicken broth to boil.
- Combine remaining ingredients in a large mixing bowl.
- Fold together until just blended. Do not over-mix.
- When the broth is boiling, add the bread crumb mixture to the broth and stir lightly.
- Cover the pot and bring back to a boil.
- Ladle into hot serving bowls.

Bueno Appetito!

Always do right; this will gratify some people and astonish the rest.

Mark Twain

Soups, Salads & Pasta

BELLA ROMA
5239 Ocean Blvd., Siesta Key

ZUPPE DI PESCE ALLE LAZIALE
Chef Flavio Cristofoli

Serves 4-8

1	small fillet of snapper
2	lobster tails
8	large shrimp
8	crab claws
8	mussels
8	oz. squid (optional)
1	clove garlic
1	pinch red peppers
1	small bunch fresh parsley, chopped
16	oz. fish stock or clam juice
6	oz. tomato sauce
1	glass white wine
1	loaf Italian bread
	salt and pepper

◆ Cut into fourths all the seafood listed above.

◆ In olive oil, sautee the garlic clove and the red pepper flakes. When garlic turns a golden color remove from heat and save.

◆ Coat bottom of large sauce pan with olive oil. Put all seafood in the large sauce pan.

◆ Sprinkle wine over seafood and add the tomato sauce, fish stock, parsley, salt and pepper.

◆ Cover and cook slowly over low heat for 15-20 minutes.

◆ Cut the Italian bread into 16 thick slices.

◆ Coat each slice with olive oil, garlic, and salt and pepper.

◆ Bake in oven until bread is crispy.

◆ Put two slices of bread on each plate, cover with seafood.

MARINA JACK II
2 Marina Place, Sarasota

CRAWFISH ETOUFEE
Frank Cappalino

Serves 4

1	med. white onion, small dice
3	celery sticks, small dice
1	garlic clove, chopped fine
¼	cup brandy
½	cup white wine
1-1½	cups chicken stock
2	Tbs. paprika
¼	cup Dijon mustard
1	Tbs. tomato paste
	cayenne pepper to taste
2	Tbs. chopped parsley
1	Tbs. green peppercorns
12	oz. crawfish tails, cooked

- Saute onion, garlic, and celery in butter for 3 minutes.
- Add brandy and white wine.
- Bring to a boil then strain.
- Set aside the vegetables.
- Add the liquid to the chicken stock with the paprika, mustard, and tomato paste.
- Thicken with a roux to the consistency of heavy cream.
- Add cayenne pepper to taste.
- Add crawfish, vegetables, parsley, and peppercorns.
- Stir and simmer for 5-10 minutes.
- Serve with white rice.

Soups, Salads & Pasta

Patricks

1442 Main Street, Sarasota

Patricks Sunday Brunch Oyster Soup

Chef Milton Linscott

Serves 6

3	stalks celery
1	Spanish onion
1	pt. fresh oysters
1	pt. water
1	pt. milk
1	pt. half and half

- ◆ Saute onion and celery in butter.
- ◆ Add oysters and cook until plump.
- ◆ Drain juice.
- ◆ Add to the juice in a saucepan the water, milk, and half and half.
- ◆ Heat and thicken with flour and butter roux.
- ◆ Add: 1 tsp. Worcestershire
         1 tsp. chicken base (bouillon)
- ◆ Add sauteed celery, onion, and oysters back into pot.

Soups, Salads & Pasta

"THE INNER CIRCLE"
1435 Main Street, Sarasota

CALIFORNIA STYLE CIOPPINO
Bleu Vorrasi

Makes two large servings

Ingredients for sauce:

- 4 large ripe tomatoes peeled, cored, seeded, and diced
- 3 cloves garlic, minced
- 1 cup dry white wine
- 2 cups fish stock (clam juice in a pinch)
- 6 fresh basil leaves, chopped
  A pinch of fresh oregano, thyme, fennel, coriander, crushed black pepper
- 2 oz. fresh parsley, coarsely chopped
- 1 large green pepper, thinly sliced
- 1 large Spanish onion, sliced thin
- 1 large portobello mushroom, sliced thin
- 1 large carrot, peeled, and sliced thin

Seafood:

- 1 lb. Alaskan crab legs, cut to 4" lengths
- 8 large shrimp, peeled and deveined
- ¼ lb. sea scallops
- ½ lb. grouper filet, cut into 1" pieces
- ½ lb. yellow fin tuna cut into 1" pieces
- 1 lb. cultured mussels, scrubbed and debearded
- 1 lb. little neck clams, scrubbed

◆ Heat 2 ounces olive oil in a 2 quart pot. Add tomato, pepper, onion, mushroom, and carrot, saute until limp.

◆ Add wine, fish stock, garlic, and herbs and let simmer 15 minutes. Turn flame to high, add seafood and cover for 7 minutes.

◆ Uncover, turn off heat and stir gently.

◆ Divide into 2 large soup bowls and top with chopped parsley. Serve hot.

Soups, Salads & Pasta

MAIN BAR
1944 Main Street, Sarasota

VEGETARIAN CHILI
Family Recipe

Makes approx. 2 quarts

Saute in ¼ cup olive oil
1	large eggplant
3	medium zucchini
2	Spanish onions
3	green peppers
1	red pepper
1	head garlic, minced

Add:
3	(28 oz.) cans Pope tomatoes
1	cup fresh parsley
1½	Tbs. chili powder
¾	tsp. cumin
½	tsp. oregano
½	tsp. basil
½	tsp. black pepper
¼	tsp. cayenne pepper
1	tsp. salt
2¼	cups garbanzo beans
1	(15 oz.) can northern beans, drained
1	(30 oz.) can kidney beans, drained
	end of one lemon (remove before serving)
1	bay leaf
¼	cup beer

◆ Serve over rice with grated cheddar cheese and scallions, small tossed salad, and a Cuban roll.

Soups, Salads & Pasta

Sarasota Brewing Company
6607 Gateway Avenue, Sarasota

Blackbeards Blackbean Gator Chili
House Recipe

Serves 12

1	gallon chicken stock
8	oz. favorite dark beer
2	cups black beans
1	med. onion, diced
2	green peppers, diced
2	red peppers, diced
4	fresh jalepenos, sliced thin
1½	lb. gator meat, chopped fine
4	Tbs. Durkees hot sauce
1	Tbs. granulated garlic
4	Tbs. chili powder
1	Tbs. cumin
½	cup butter
½	cup flour

- Rinse beans well and soak in chicken stock and beer for 24 hours in a large soup pot.
- Bring beans and spices to a slow boil for 1½ hours.
- Saute peppers, onions, and gator meat until done.
- Add chicken stock and simmer all of the above for one more hour.
- Thicken with a semi-dark roux.

At Sarasota Brewing Co., they use Blackbeards Dark beer, hence the name.

Soups, Salads & Pasta

WILDFLOWER NATURAL FOOD RESTAURANT

5218 Ocean Blvd., Siesta Key

MEDITERRANEAN BURRITOS
Chef Marc Henri

Serves 8

2	cups cooked black beans, mashed
1	tsp. cumin powder
1	clove garlic, minced
2	Tbs. minced fresh cilantro
½	Tbs. chili powder
	a pinch of salt
8	whole wheat flour tortillas
2	cups Salsa
2	cups feta cheese, crumbled
2	cups fresh tomatoes, diced
½	cup black olives, sliced
½	cup chopped red onions

- ◆ Mix together black beans, cumin, garlic, cilantro, chili powder, and salt.
- ◆ Heat tortillas according to package directions.
- ◆ Divide bean mixture among tortillas and roll them up.
- ◆ Place tortillas on individual serving dishes.
- ◆ Top with Salsa then cheese, tomatoes, olives, and onions.

Soups, Salads & Pasta

THE CHART HOUSE
201 Gulf of Mexico Drive, Longboat Key

CHART HOUSE BLEU CHEESE DRESSING
Dave Lynch

Makes 2½ cups

¾	cup sour cream
½	tsp. dry mustard
½	tsp. black pepper
½	tsp. salt (optional)
⅓	tsp. garlic powder,
1	tsp. Worcestershire sauce

1⅓	cups mayonnaise
4	oz. crumbled imported Danish bleu cheese

◆ In a mixing bowl, combine first 6 ingredients and blend for 2 minutes at low speed.

◆ Add mayonnaise and blend ½ minute at low speed, then increase speed to medium and blend an additional 2 minutes.

◆ Slowly add bleu cheese and blend at low speed no longer than 4 minutes.

◆ Refrigerate for 24 hours before serving.

Soups, Salads & Pasta

COLUMBIA
St. Armands Circle, Sarasota

1905 SALAD

Serves 4 dinner salads or 2 main entrees

- ½ head iceberg lettuce
- 2 tomatoes, diced
- 1 celery stalk, diced
- 3 oz. Swiss cheese, julienned
- 3 oz. ham, julienned
- ¼ cup pitted Spanish olives
- 2 Tbs. Romano cheese

Dressing: (the most important part):
- 4 garlic cloves, minced
- 1 tsp. oregano
- 1 tsp. Worcestershire sauce
- ½ cup olive oil
  juice of ½ a lemon
- ⅛ cup white vinegar
  salt and pepper

◆ Arrange salad ingredients in serving bowl or individual salad plates.
◆ To prepare dressing, mince garlic and put into a bowl.
◆ Add oregano, Worcestershire sauce, and lemon juice.
◆ Beat with a wire whisk until smooth.
◆ Add the oil gradually and finally add the vinegar beating continuously.
◆ Add salt and pepper to taste.
◆ When well-mixed, pour dressing over salad and toss.

Insomniac's Coffee House & Cafe

6592 Superior Ave., Sarasota

Tropical Chicken Salad

Janice Presley

Serves 25

  8   chicken breasts or more
  2   tsp. salt
  4   Tbs. orange juice
  4   Tbs. salad oil
  4   Tbs. vinegar

◆ Boil chicken, cool, cube or flake. Mix above ingredients and pour over chicken, mix well and refrigerate covered overnight.

  3   cups raw rice

◆ Cook rice until tender. Don't drain, cover and refrigerate overnight.

  3   cups chunk pineapple, drain and refrigerate
  3   cups mandarin oranges, drain and refrigerate
  3   cups red and green seedless grapes, wash, drain and refrigerate
  3   cups celery, chop and refrigerate
  2   cups sliced almonds

◆ Place each one of these in separate covered containers overnight in refrigerator. It might seem silly, but it really does make it better!

◆ The next day, about 2 hours before serving, drain rice and chicken.

◆ Combine all the ingredients together in a very large bowl. Mix together with just enough mayonnaise to coat. Mayonnaise will be about 1 qt.

◆ To serve, place salad on lettuce leaves. Sprinkle raisins on top and perhaps a few more almonds.

◆ Serve with slice melon, berries, and dinner rolls.

Great for wedding or baby showers.

BANYAN

John and Mable Ringling Museum of Art, Sarasota

SMOKED CHICKEN AND APPLE SALAD

Dennis Cole

Serves 6

¾	lb. smoked chicken, cut into 1" pieces
1	medium red bell pepper, cut julienne
2	large Granny Smith apples, peeled, cored, and cut into ½" slices
1	cup pecans
1	small red onion, thinly sliced
1	small garlic clove, minced
¼	tsp. dry sage
1	Tbs. Dijon mustard
1	Tbs. white wine vinegar
¼	tsp. salt
¼	tsp. freshly ground black pepper
⅓	cup extra virgin olive oil

◆ Preheat oven to 400°.

◆ Spread pecans on baking sheet and cook in the oven until fragrant, about 5 minutes. Let cool and crumble into smaller pieces.

◆ In a small bowl combine garlic, sage, mustard, vinegar, salt, and pepper.

◆ Slowly whisk in olive oil.

◆ Put onion slices in a small bowl. Cover with cold water and soak for 7 to 10 minutes. Drain well.

◆ In a large bowl, combine onion, apples, red pepper, and chicken.

◆ Pour the vinaigrette over the salad and toss well.

◆ Divide the salad onto 6 chilled plates, sprinkle with toasted pecans and serve.

HARRY'S CONTINENTAL KITCHENS
525 St. Judes Dr., Longboat Key

HOT FLOUNDER SALAD
OVER WILTED SPINACH
Harry Christensen

Serves 6

1	cup olive oil
2	lbs. flounder fillets, cut into 3" pieces
2	rounded Tbs. finely chopped shallots
2	cups diced, peeled and seeded tomatoes
½	cup fresh lemon juice
2	Tbs. sugar
1	Tbs. coarsely chopped fresh basil
¼	cup white wine
¾-1	lb. fresh spinach
	chopped scallions and sliced, toasted almonds
	flour, salt and pepper for dredging

- ◆ Wash and dry spinach. Divide spinach into six serving bowls.
- ◆ Dust flounder with flour, salt, and pepper.
- ◆ Saute fish in hot olive oil until lightly browned, turning once to cook thoroughly and brown evenly.
- ◆ Drain and arrange pieces over spinach.
- ◆ Add shallots to the hot oil remaining in the pan, stir a few seconds, and add tomatoes, lemon juice, sugar, and basil. Stir together and add wine.
- ◆ Boil rapidly two to three minutes. Tomatoes should be cooked through but remain firm.
- ◆ Spoon sauce over and around fillets and spinach.
- ◆ Garnish with chopped scallions and toasted almonds.
- ◆ Serve hot for a first course, luncheon entree or a light supper.

Soups, Salads & Pasta

SHELLS
7253 South Tamiami Trail, Sarasota

SEAFOOD PASTA
Serves 4

For Pasta:
1   lb. linguine
1   oz. butter
    salt

Cook linguine in salt water with butter until al dente, drain and set aside.

Seafood Mix:
4   oz. mussel meat
6   oz. chopped clams, cooked and drained
10   oz. raw scallops
10   oz. peeled raw shrimp

Sauce:
4   oz. olive oil
4   oz. dry cooking wine
8   cloves fresh garlic, finely chopped
     salt and pepper to taste

◆ Combine sauce ingredients in a sauce pan and bring to a boil.
◆ Add seafood, mix and stir gently for two minutes.
◆ Lower heat and add cooked linguine.
◆ Stir gently, approximately 10 minutes, or until seafood is done and dish has a creamy consistency.
◆ Serve immediately!

NEPTUNES
5238 Ocean Blvd., Siesta Key

SEAFOOD PRIMAVERA
Chef Steven King

Serves 6-8

3	cups heavy cream
1½	cups strong chicken broth
2	Tbs. minced garlic
8	oz. Parmesan cheese
4	egg yolks
2	lb. cooked linguine
1½	heads broccoli
3	large carrots
1	Bermuda onion
1	red pepper
½	lb. crab meat
1	lb. shrimp
1	lb. scallops
2	cups white wine
	juice of 2 lemons
¾	lb. butter

- ◆ In a sauce pan heat first three ingredients until reduced by one third. Add Parmesan slowly until thoroughly blended.
- ◆ Remove from heat and stir in egg yolks quickly. Mix sauce with linguine, keep warm.
- ◆ Julienne vegetables and poach with seafood in white wine and lemon juice, stirring occasionally to insure even cooking.
- ◆ Remove from heat and slowly incorporate butter one ounce at a time.
- ◆ Serve over linguine and enjoy.

THE SERVING SPOON
1825 South Osprey Ave., Sarasota

PEANUT PASTA SALAD
James Palermo

Serves 8-12

Peanut Sauce:
- ¼ cup tea (cooled)
- ¼ cup soy sauce
- ½ cup peanut oil
- ¼ cup brown sugar
- 1 cup peanut butter (crunchy or creamy)
- 2 cloves of garlic (chopped fine)
- 1 tsp. fresh ginger root (peeled and chopped fine)
- dash or two of tabasco sauce
- dash or two of Worcestershire sauce

Mix sauce by combining all ingredients. Can be made a day or two ahead of time.

Salad ingredients:
- 1 red pepper
- 1 green pepper
- 1 small zucchini
- 1 small yellow squash
- ½ lbs. mushrooms
- 1 small onion
- 1 lb. boneless skinless chicken breast (cut into strips)
- 1 lb. pasta (chef's choice, they all work well)
- 1 lg. head romaine lettuce
- 1 jar roasted peanuts (unsalted)

Soups, Salads & Pasta

- ◆ Chop all the vegetables in one inch pieces and mix together.
- ◆ Cook pasta al dente, drain, and toss with a couple Tbs. of peanut oil, keep warm.
- ◆ While pasta is cooking saute vegetables in 4 Tbs. of peanut oil, reserve.
- ◆ Saute chicken in 4 Tbs. of peanut oil until golden brown, add cooked vegetables and stir well.
- ◆ Add cooked pasta and combine.
- ◆ Add ½ of the peanut sauce and stir.
- ◆ Continue to add sauce little by little until desired consistency.
- ◆ Serve on a bed of chopped romaine lettuce and garnish with roasted peanuts.

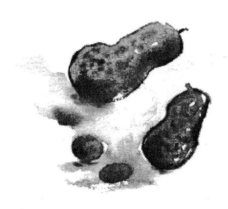

Soups, Salads & Pasta

Main Bar
1944 Main St., Sarasota

Pasta Minestrone
Family Recipe

Makes 1 large pasta bowl

The night before: Cook 1½ lb. Penne pasta. Marinate in Italian dressing to coat. Add an extra tablespoon of oregano, basil, and granulated garlic.

The next day: Start steamer with a teaspoon of oregano, basil, salt, pepper, and granulated garlic. Steam separately:

1	lb. carrots, quartered and diced
½	lb. green beans, bite size
2	med. zucchini, small dice
½	lb. peas

Chop by hand:

½	red onion
¼	bunch parsley

Toss all with pasta, adding:
1-15 oz. can dark red kidney beans, drained
   2 cups garbanzo beans, drained and rinsed
Add enough Italian dressing to coat.
Add 1 cup Parmesan cheese. Garnish with tomato slice and parsley.

CHEF CALDWELL'S
20 South Adams Drive, St. Armands Circle

VEGETARIAN ANGEL HAIR
Chef Frank Caldwell

Serve 8

Vegetable cooking spray
2   tsp. olive oil
1   cup fresh broccoli flowerets
1   cup fresh cauliflower flowerets
1   cup julienned carrots
1   cup julienned zucchini
1   Tbs. + 1 tsp. minced garlic
1   cup snow pea pods, trimmed
¼   cup canned (no salt added) chicken broth
1   cup cherry tomatoes, halved
8   oz. angel hair, uncooked
2   Tbs. pine nuts, toasted
2   Tbs. parsley, chopped

◆ Coat a large nonstick skillet with cooking spray; add oil.

◆ Place over medium high heat until hot.

◆ Add broccoli, cauliflower, carrot, zucchini and garlic; saute 4 minutes. Stir in snow peas and chicken broth. Cover, reduce heat and cook 6 minutes.

◆ Stir in tomato halves and cook an additional 3 minutes.

◆ Cook pasta according to package directions, omitting salt and fat; drain.

◆ Add pasta to vegetable mixture, tossing well.

◆ Sprinkle in pine nuts and parsley.

◆ Serve immediately!

BELLINIS RISTORANTE
1549 Main Street, Downtown Sarasota

FETTUCCINE ALLA SICILIANA
Serves 6

1	large eggplant
½	cup of olive oil
2	cloves of garlic, crushed
6	large ripe tomatoes, ½" dice
2	green pepper, ½" dice
3-4	anchovy fillets
½	cup black olives, pitted and halved
4	tsp. capers
2-3	sprigs of finely chopped basil
1½	lb. fettuccine, cooked

◆ Peel and cube eggplant.

◆ Saute in oil and garlic until tender.

◆ Add remaining ingredients and simmer.

◆ When ready toss sauce with fettuccine and serve.

PICCOLO MONDO
3131 Clark Road, Sarasota

LINGUINE AND STAGIONI
Carlo Tonelli

Serves 8

Chill one large mixing bowl

- 2 lb. dry linguine
- 1 cup olive oil
- 2 tsp. red wine vinegar
- 8 tsp. Parmesan cheese, freshly grated
- 2½ tsp. black pepper
- 2½ tsp. fresh chopped garlic
- 2 tsp. fresh chopped basil
- 2 tsp. fresh chopped parsley
- 2 cups diced tomatoes
- 1 cup diced onion

◆ Bring a large pot of water to a rolling boil. Cook pasta until done and drain well.

◆ In chilled mixing bowl, combine the above ingredients. Mix well. Add the cooked pasta and toss together.

◆ Serve in warm bowls. This dish is meant to be served at room temperature, not hot.

CAFE BACI
4001 S. Tamiami Trail, Sarasota

CAVATAPPI PAPALINI
Roberto and Denise Mei

Serves 6-8

1   lb. spiral or Rigatoni pasta cooked al dente in salted
    water
1   lb. fresh mushrooms sliced. Saute in a little butter and
    set aside.
15 strips of bacon or pancetta cut into pieces. Fry and set
    aside.
4   Tbs. frozen peas taken from bag.

1   stick of butter
1   tsp. of bacon grease
1   cup of heavy cream
½   cup of half and half
    grated Parmesan cheese

◆ In a large frying pan combine the above 4 ingredients,
  bring to a boil. As soon as mixture starts to boil add
  grated Parmesan cheese until mixture coats a wooden
  spoon.
◆ While still boiling add bacon, mushrooms, and peas, stir
  together and pour over pasta.
◆ Add a little pepper to taste.

This recipe has been handed down through 5 generations of
Roberto's family.

Nick's On The Water
230 Sarasota Quay, Sarasota

Rigatoni Ala Vodka
Janet Allen

Serves 8

½	onion, Spanish or white
3	slices boiled ham
1	can 28 oz. Progresso whole tomatoes with basil
1	can 15½ oz. Hunts tomato sauce
1	(6 oz.) can Hunts tomato paste
1	clove of garlic, diced
1	Tbs. parsley
2	tsp. basil
½	tsp. crushed red pepper
½	tsp. cayenne pepper
3-5	oz. domestic vodka
3	oz. fresh Parmesan cheese
1½- to 3	oz. whole cream
1	lb. Rigatoni pasta
2	Tbs. butter

◆ In a food processor, puree onion and dice ham very fine. Empty whole tomatoes into mixing bowl and squeeze with fingers.

◆ Put 1 Tbs. of olive oil in saute pan. Place over medium heat. Add onion and ham and saute for approximately 1½ minutes.

◆ Add whole tomatoes, tomato sauce, tomato paste, garlic, parsley, basil, crushed red pepper, cayenne pepper, and 3 oz. of the vodka.

◆ Cook for 20-25 minutes over medium heat to reduce.

◆ Add cream and cheese. Stir thoroughly.

◆ Add the remaining vodka according to taste and thickness.

◆ Reduce heat to low and allow to simmer 5 minutes.

◆ To finish, add butter; stir through, and serve over Rigatoni.

Soups, Salads & Pasta

CARAGIULOS
69 South Palm Avenue, Sarasota

CHICKEN VEGETABLE LASAGNA IN PARMESAN CUSTARD

Serves 6-8

Custard:

1	stick butter
½	cup plus 2 Tbs. flour
4	cups milk
2	cups chicken stock
6	whole eggs
1	cup grated Parmesan cheese
	salt to taste
	pinch of ground red pepper
	pinch of ground nutmeg

20	lasagna noodles
2	Tbs. butter
1	chopped onion
1	garlic clove, minced
3	whole boneless chicken breasts cut into ¼ inch strips
1	lb. blanched broccoli, chopped
½	cup shredded carrot
½	cup sliced mushrooms
½	lb. fresh spinach
1	lb. sliced or shredded mozzarella
½	cup grated Parmesan cheese
¼	cup chopped Italian flat leaf parsley

- To make custard, melt butter in medium saucepan.
- Stir in flour, over low heat, until smooth and golden. Stir in milk, whisk over medium heat until smooth. Stir in chicken stock. Cook until thick and smooth.
- Beat the eggs in a separate bowl, gradually whisk sauce into eggs, return to saucepan and let stand off heat.
- Stir in cheese, season with salt, pepper, and nutmeg.
- After cooking lasagna noodles al dente, let noodles sit in a bowl of cool water until ready to use.
- Melt 2 Tbs. butter in large skillet. Add onion, saute until golden. Stir in the garlic, saute 1 minute.
- Add chicken strips, cook for 2 minutes then add carrot, broccoli, mushrooms, and spinach.
- Cook until tender. Season with salt and pepper.
- In a 9" x 13" baking dish spoon about 1 cup custard into bottom of baking dish.
- Arrange dry noodles slightly overlapping.
- Arrange ½ the chicken vegetable mixture over the noodles.
- Drizzle with 1 cup of custard.
- Add layer of ⅓ the mozzarella. Sprinkle with 2 Tbs. Parmesan cheese.
- Arrange second layer of lasagna noodles and repeat.
- Top last layer of lasagna with remaining mozzarella, Parmesan and custard.
- Cover baking dish tightly with aluminum foil.
- Bake 350° approx. 1 hour and let stand at least 20 minutes before serving.

Soups, Salads & Pasta

Pasta Del Giorno
2085 Siesta Drive, Sarasota

Linguine Alla Puttanesca
Fresh Egg Linguine with Puttanesca Sauce
Chef Angelo Cori

Serves 4

2	Tbs. olive oil
3	garlic cloves, thinly sliced
¼	tsp. hot pepper flakes
6	flat anchovy fillets, finely chopped
4	oz. imported black olives
4	oz. imported green olives
1	Tbs. capers, rinsed and drained
1	28 oz. can Italian peeled tomatoes, drained and chopped
½	tsp. salt
¼	tsp. pepper
1	lb. fresh egg linguine

◆ In a large frying pan, heat olive oil over medium heat. Stir in garlic, hot pepper flakes and anchovies. Cook about 1 minute, until fragrant.

◆ Add olives, capers and tomatoes. Cook, stirring occasionally, until sauce thickens. Season with salt and pepper.

◆ Bring large pot of water to boil. Add linguine and cook for just 3 minutes.

◆ Pour pasta and sauce into large warmed bowl and toss together.

The Oaks

Photo courtesy of Historic Spanish Point

◆ Chapter Three ◆

Meats & Poultry

Mrs. Potter Palmer
and The Oaks

Mrs. Potter Palmer's arrival to Sarasota changed not only the social scene but the cattle ranching industry. In 1910, Mrs. Palmer, a Chicago socialite who had traveled the world and owned homes in London and Paris, was told Sarasota was the finest place in the world to live — a place where one could make very profitable investments.

Her decision to visit the Sarasota area caused a stir among those involved in attracting her to this region. They quickly realized there was no suitable hotel in Sarasota to house this well known guest. Oddly, Dr. Jack Halton's sanitarium on Gulf Stream Avenue, being the best equipped building in town, was quickly renovated and refurbished. This undertaking proved a good investment; Mrs. Potter Palmer was impressed with her accommodations and the "refreshingly quaint" town.

On a sight seeing trip, Mrs. Potter was shown an area where a cabbage palm and an oak tree had become entwined in such a way that they looked like one single tree. This special tree, the lands surrounding it, and the view of the bay in Osprey, was enough to sell Mrs. Palmer the area. She bought the property immediately to situate her winter home.

This thirteen acre tract of land was known as "The Oaks" (now "Historic Spanish Point"). Eventually she expanded her estate to 140,000 acres, part of which she donated to Sarasota county for what now is Myakka State Park.

Mrs. Palmer introduced cattle dipping to combat tick disease in her herd. Other ranchers at first resisted the technique until they realized its effectiveness. She eventually expanded her agricultural operations with a citrus grove and celery farm operation.

Historic Spanish Point, an environmental, archaeological and Historic National Register site, is open to the public. Call 813-966-5214 for information.

Mrs. Potter Palmer

BANYAN
John and Mable Ringling Museum of Art, Sarasota

GRILLED LAMB CHOPS AND LINGUINE WITH MINT PESTO
Chef Denis Cole

Serves 6

12-2"	thick lamb chops
½	cup fresh lemon juice
2	Tbs. freshly grated lemon rind
¼	cup freshly chopped thyme leaves
¼	cup chopped shallots
2	tsp. salt
1	tsp. freshly ground pepper
½	cup vegetable oil
12	oz. pkg. linguine, cooked al dente

◆ Mix above ingredients thoroughly and marinate lamb chops over night in the refrigerator.

◆ Remove the lamb chops from marinade, pat them dry and grill to preferred taste (about 5 minutes per side for medium).

◆ Serve with linguine. Season with the mint pesto.

Mint Pesto:

4	cups firmly packed fresh mint leaves
2	Tbs. chopped walnuts
½	tsp. minced garlic
½	tsp. salt
½	cup olive oil
½	cup freshly grated Parmesan cheese.

◆ In a blender or food processor, combine the above ingredients until smooth. Add to the hot pasta and serve.

OLD HEIDELBERG CASTLE
Third Street and Route 301, Sarasota

JAGERSCHNITZEL
Chef Michael Ostermann

Serves 4

◆ Take 4 thin veal loin chops, season with salt and pepper. Turn them in flour and saute in hot butter.

Add:

 3 *oz. Chablis wine*
 8 *oz. sliced mushrooms*
    chopped parsley and onions

◆ Season mixture with salt, pepper, and garlic.
◆ Simmer covered for 8 minutes.
◆ Remove chops from pan and finish sauce with a little heavy cream and a dash of lemon juice.

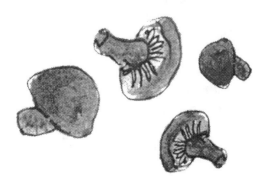

BELLINI RISTORANTE
1549 Main Street, Downtown Sarasota

VEAL SCALLOPINI WITH ENDIVES

Serves 6

1½   *lb. of veal scallopini*
     They should be as thin as possible and may be
     pounded. Dredge veal in flour and saute in:
4   *Tbs. sweet butter and*
2   *Tbs. olive oil*

◆ Heat until fragrant, and juices begin to emerge in the
   upper side. Turn the veal and continue to saute for about
   3 minutes more.

◆ Shake the pan vigorously from time to time, until the
   meat is done.

◆ If all your veal will not fit in your saute pan keep the
   already finished cutlets uncovered in a 250° oven until all
   the rest are ready.

   Deglaze the pan juices with:
   ¾   *cup Marsala wine*
       freshly ground salt and pepper
       pinch of thyme

◆ Arrange veal on top of Belgian endive.

◆ Pour sauce over veal.

◆ Garnish with lemon, slice and serve at once.

BELLA ROMA
5239 Ocean Blvd., Siesta Key

OSSO BUCO ALLA MILANESE
Chef Flavio Cristofoli

Serves 4

4	veal shanks cut 3" thick
2	oz. butter
2	garlic cloves
½	large onion chopped
	white wine (you may substitute chicken or a beef broth
	flour to dredge
1	fresh tomato chopped (optional)
	salt and pepper

Gremolata sauce:

2	oz. fresh parsley
	zest of ½ a lemon
	garlic
	onion
2	anchovy fillets, mashed

◆ In a large ovenproof pan, saute garlic cloves and onion in 2 oz. butter. When garlic cloves turn a golden brown, remove garlic and onions from pan and save.

◆ Flour the veal shanks and brown on both sides.

◆ Reduce heat and cook slowly. Sprinkle with white wine or broth and add chopped tomato if you like.

◆ Add salt and pepper, cover and cook in 375° oven for 1½ hours.

◆ Prepare the gremolata sauce. Mix parsley, sauteed garlic, onion and zest of lemon with the mashed anchovy.

◆ When veal shanks are ready, spread gremolata sauce on top and serve.

Flavio suggests a nice bottle of Barberra wine to complement.

LIMERICK JUNCTION PUB AND CLUB
1296 First Street, downtown Sarasota

SHEPHERDS PIE
Michael Gordan

Serves 6

3	Tbs. flour
2	cups beef bouillon
2	lb. ground beef
½	cup minced onion
½	cup minced carrot
8	medium potatoes, peeled
3	Tbs. minced chives
2	Tbs. butter

- ◆ Boil potatoes until tender.
- ◆ Saute the beef, onions, and carrots until brown.
- ◆ Drain off fat. Add 3 Tbs. flour and 2 cups rich beef stock.
- ◆ Simmer until thickened. Season with granulated garlic, Worcestershire, salt and pepper to taste.
- ◆ Whip potatoes with 3 Tbs. minced chives, 2 Tbs. butter, salt and pepper to taste.
- ◆ Place sauted beef in casserole dish.
- ◆ Put whipped potatoes in pastry bag with star tip. Pipe onto beef making neat rows on top. Brown under broiler.

TUDOR ROSE
3676 Webber Street, Sarasota

CORNISH PASTIES

Serves 4-6

8	oz. pastry dough (a reg. 2 crust pie recipe will do fine)
8	oz. of diced lamb or beef
2	oz. raw potato
2	oz. raw diced carrots
1	oz. peas
1	diced onion
	salt and pepper

◆ Make pastry. Cut large rounds with a saucer or tea plate.

◆ Chop or mince meat. Peel potatoes, onions, and carrots and dice finely. Mix meat and vegetables together adding salt and pepper.

◆ Place mixture in the center of the pastry rounds, sprinkling with a little water. Brush edges with water. Bring edges together over filling. Press together gently and flute edges. Make sure pastie is completely sealed so that the steam cannot escape and contents cook in their own juices.

◆ Cook in a hot oven (425° - 450°) for 15 minutes, then lower temperature a little and cook for a full 30-35 minutes.

What one does, one becomes.
Spanish Proverb

OSTERIA
29½ N. Blvd. of the Presidents, St. Armands Circle

BEEF BRACIOLE
Stuffed Rolled Beef served with Penne Pasta

Chef Frank Bologno

Serves 4

1½	lb. top round of beef (cut into 6 oz. slices)
4	thin slices of prosciutto
¼	cup cilantro, chopped fine
¼	cup fresh basil, chopped coarse
4	hard boiled eggs cut into quarters
1	cup Parmesan cheese
¼	Tbs. minced garlic
¼	cup pine nuts

Sauce:

½	stalk celery, large dice
2	carrots, large dice
3	onions, large dice
3	oz. pancetta (round Italian bacon)
8	whole peeled Italian tomatoes
2	cups dry red wine
2	oz. Marsala wine
2	Bay leaves
	salt and pepper to taste
2	cloves garlic
2	Tbs. basil
2	Tbs. cilantro
¾	lb. of Penne (tubular pasta)

◆ Place slices of beef between 2 sheets of lightly oiled wax paper and pound beef paper thin.

◆ Place beef slices on flat surface, season with salt and pepper. Top each beef slice with a slice of prosciutto.

- Combine garlic, basil, Parmesan, eggs, pine nuts, and cilantro. Divide this stuffing mixture equally on each slice of beef. Roll each slice into a neat bundle and tie securely with kitchen string.

- Heat a heavy skillet over medium high heat. Cover bottom with a thin coat of oil. Brown beef rolls on all sides, then set aside.

- Add celery, carrots, onions, garlic, bay leaf, basil, cilantro, and lightly saute.

- Deglaze skillet with red wine and Marsala wine. Add tomatoes and pancetta.

- Strain the sauce through a china cap (fine mesh screen), while the beef bundles cool for 20 minutes. Remove string. Gently add beef bundles to sauce.

- Cook Penne al dente.

- Take some of your sauce and saute a little with the Penne pasta. Place Penne on each plate.

- Take about 4 Tbs. of the sauce and put it on the plate, placing the cut Braciole on top. Top with a little more sauce, Parmesan cheese, and basil.

THE INNER CIRCLE
1435 Main Street, Sarasota

ERNESTO'S TOURNADOS ROSSINI
Bleu Vorrasi

A Special Dinner for Two

4	*(3 oz.) filet mignons*
4	*(1 oz.) slices duck liver pate*
½	*cup demi-glace**
¼	*cup Maderia or sweet port wine*
12	*poached asparagus spears*
8	*oz. cooked crab leg meat (whole and shelled)*
1	*cup Bernaise sauce*
4	*toasted 3" diameter croutons (¼ inch thick)*

◆ Heat saute pan over high heat. Add 2 oz. olive oil to pan. To hot oil, add lightly floured beef medallions. Brown on both sides and drain oil from pan.

◆ Place 2 medallions per plate atop toasted croutons.

◆ Return hot pan to stove and add wine to boil. Add demi-glace to pan and simmer until reduced by half. Add crab, asparagus, and pate to reduction until warm.

◆ Place one slice of pate atop each medallion and top each pate with 3 spears of heated asparagus.

◆ Top asparagus with 2 oz. crab meat.

◆ Pour the sauce that is left in the pan over each medallion and finish with a 2 oz. dollop of Bernaise sauce on each serving.

◆ Garnish with freshly chopped parsley, serve hot.

*Demi-glace is a very stong beef or veal stock.

CHEF CALDWELLS
20 South Adams Drive, St. Armands Circle

GRILLED PORK LOIN *with a Raspberry Barbeque Sauce*
Chef Frank Caldwell

Serves 8
This is a heart healthy dish approved by Heart Center of
Sarasota. Figure on a 6 oz. pork loin per person

For Raspberry Barbeque Sauce:

8	oz. can no salt tomato sauce
¾	cup chopped red onion
½	cup + 2 Tbs. no salt chili sauce
½	cup raspberry vinegar
1	Tbs. honey
1	tsp. low sodium Worcestershire sauce
1	clove garlic, minced
½	tsp. dry mustard
½	tsp. cinnamon
¼	tsp. ground cloves
⅛	tsp. ginger

For marinate: Combine 1 cup peanut oil with 1 cup raspberry
vinegar. Salt and pepper to taste.

◆ Cut and pound pork loin into 3 oz. medallions. Place in
shallow pan with marinade. Marinate 1 hour turning
pork halfway through.

◆ While marinating, prepare raspberry sauce. Combine
first 6 ingredients in saucepan. Add garlic, mustard,
cinnamon, cloves, and ginger. Bring to a boil; reduce and
simmer 10 minutes.

◆ Remove pork from marinade. Grill or bake 3 minutes
per side, brushing with raspberry sauce while cooking.

◆ Serve with applesauce and steamed potatoes.

Roessler's Flight Deck
2033 Vamo Way, Sarasota

Cherry Duckling
Claus Roessler

Serves 2-3

1	3-3½ lb. Long Island duck
2	whole Bay leaves
2	white onions, chopped
3	stalks celery, chopped 1" pieces
	salt and pepper to taste
½	cup melted butter
3	Tbs. sifted flour
2	cups chicken stock
½	cup pitted dark sweet cherries, with juice (canned cherries will work).
3	Tbs. cherry liquor
3	Tbs. brandy

◆ Wipe duck with a damp cloth. Stuff duck with Bay leaves, onion, and celery. Salt and pepper duck and place in roasting pan. Brush duck with melted butter. Roast in a preheated oven at 475° for 30-45 minutes. To check duck, pierce with a fork - if juice runs clear, the duck is done. Remove from pan and keep warm while preparing sauce.

Sauce:

◆ Stir flour into pan drippings and brown.

◆ Blend in chicken stock and bring to a boil, approx. 10 minutes.

◆ Remove from heat and strain into sauce pan.

◆ Add cherries and simmer 3-5 minutes. Add cherry liquor and brandy.

◆ Serve sauce with duckling, wild rice, and vegetable of your choice for a wonderful dinner!

CHEZ SYLVIE
1526 Main Street, Sarasota

ROAST CORNISH HENS NORMANDY
Sylvie Routier

Serves 6

6	*(18 oz.) Cornish hens*
6	*Granny Smith apples*
4	*oz. sweet unsalted butter, melted*
½	*cup sugar*

Spice mix:

2	*Tbs. basil,*
2	*Tbs. rosemary,*
2	*Tbs. savory,*
2	*Tbs. thyme*
1	*Tbs. fennel seed*
1	*Tbs. black pepper*
1	*Tbs. salt*
6	*oz. Calvados (apple brandy)*
1	*cup heavy cream*

◆ Cut apples in half, from end to end. Remove seeds. Place apples in baking dish cut side up. Pour butter over apples then sprinkle them with sugar.

◆ Make spice mix using all the above spices except salt. Rub half the spice mix on the inside of the hens. Sprinkle the remaining spice on the hens with the salt.

◆ Roast hens 50 minutes at 375° or until done.

◆ After 25 minutes, put apples in oven and bake for 25 minutes. Apples should be tender and slightly caramelized.

◆ Remove hens and reduce juices.

◆ Heat brandy, ignite, and pour into pan juices.

◆ Add cream to finish.

◆ Serve sauce over hens and apples.

TURTLES
8875 Midnight Pass, Siesta Key

SOUTHWESTERN CHARGRILLED CHICKEN
with Grilled Zucchini and Citrus - Chili Pepper Relish
Chef Eric Brown

Serves 6

Marinade for chicken breast:

6	(8 oz.) boneless chicken breasts
1	Tbs. chopped fresh garlic
½	cup red wine vinegar
½	cup BBQ sauce
2	Tbs. soy sauce
¼	cup water
¼	cup olive oil
	juice of 4 limes

◆ Puree ingredients in blender. Marinate chicken breast overnight before grilling.

For seafood, follow same procedures but add ½ lb. melted margarine to recipe before marinating.

Citrus and Chili Pepper Relish:

1	medium red onion, ½ inch dice
2	medium tomatoes, ½ inch dice
6	oranges, peeled and ½ inch dice
3	thinly sliced Anaheim peppers
¾	cup chopped cilantro
2	Tbs. olive oil
	salt and pepper to taste

Combine ingredients in bowl.

Zucchini for Grilling:
Slice 3 zucchini in half length wise. Brush on olive oil, chopped garlic and black pepper.

◆ Grill chicken breast and zucchini over hot coals to your liking. Arrange on serving dish and top with the relish.

SANDBAR
100 Spring Avenue, Anna Maria Island

TEQUILA CHICKEN
Steve Mierzejewski

Serves 2

2	boneless, skinless chicken breasts
1	tsp. cumin
1	tsp. kosher salt
½	shot triple sec
½	shot tequila
4	slices Monterey Jack cheese
1	bag tortilla chips

Salsa
2	vine ripe tomatoes, skinned and seeded
2	Tbs. fresh chopped cilantro
1	lime, squeezed
2	Tbs. chopped jalapeno
¾	cup chopped onion

◆ Coat chicken breasts with salt and cumin. Saute breasts until brown, add triple sec and tequila. Ignite. When flame goes out or the firemen leave, whichever comes first, add ½ the salsa and put in preheated oven at 350° for 15 minutes.

◆ Remove, top with Monterey Jack. Put back in oven until the cheese is melted.

◆ On a separate plate, arrange tortilla chips and ring with the rest of the salsa. Place the chicken breast in the center of the plate and sprinkle with the jalapeno peppers.

Emphasis
1301 First Street, Sarasota

Chicken Florentine with Acorn Squash Sauce

Serves 4

> 1 lb. spinach
> 1 Tbs. olive oil
> 1 Tbs. crushed garlic
> 1 tsp. nutmeg
> 4-7 oz. chicken breasts with skin
> 1 cup chicken stock
> 2 acorn squash cooked and pureed
> ½ stick of butter
> salt and pepper
> ¼ lb. Swiss cheese, grated
> 1 Tbs. rubbed sage

◆ Saute spinach in olive oil and garlic, add salt, pepper and nutmeg to taste. Set aside.

◆ Pound out chicken to an even thickness. Sear chicken skin side down for one minute.

◆ Remove chicken and deglaze pan with chicken stock. Add cooked, puree of squash and bring to a simmer.

◆ Add butter 1 Tbs. at a time. Salt and pepper to taste.

◆ Place cheese and spinach mixture on half of the chicken breast and fold in half.

◆ Sprinkle with black pepper and rubbed sage to taste. Place in hot 400° oven and bake for 10 minutes.

◆ Ladle hot squash mixture on plate, on top of finished chicken. YUM!

Ciao! Casual International Cuisine
5370 Gulf of Mexico Dr., Longboat Key

Paella New Iberia
Chef Bill Shafer

Serves 6-8

One 2½-3 lb. chicken, cut into serving pieces
¾ lb. andouillle sausage, cut into ½" pieces.
8 crawfish
12 clams or mussels
1 lb. large shrimp, peeled and deveined
2 med. bell peppers, seeded, and diced
1 lg. tomato, peeled, seeded and diced
4 cloves garlic, crushed
¼ cup chopped fresh parsley or cilantro
½ tsp. saffron
1½ cups converted rice
1 cup tomato juice
1 cup clam juice
1 cup chicken broth
2 Tbs. olive oil
Louisiana hot sauce to taste
flour for dredging

◆ Preheat oven to 425°.

◆ In a saucepan, combine liquid ingredients and bring to a simmer.

◆ On high heat, in a large cast iron skillet cook chicken dredged in flour and oil until browned on all sides.

◆ Add peppers, tomato, garlic and sausage. When vegetables start to soften, add rice, saffron, salt and hot sauce. Continue to cook on high heat for 2 minutes, then carefully add simmering broth and shell fish.

◆ When full boil is reached, put skillet, uncovered, into oven.

◆ Paella is ready when chicken is cooked through and rice is done - about 20 minutes.

POKI JOE'S CAFE
6614 Superior Ave., Sarasota

POKI JOE'S FAMOUS MELODIOUS CHICKEN
Serves 4 heartily

3	(8 oz.) chicken breasts
½	large onion, sliced
½	red or green pepper, sliced
1	large handful sliced mushrooms
¾	cups grated mozzarella cheese
¾	cups mild provolone cheese
⅓	cup sliced blanched almonds
⅓	cup pecan pieces
6	Tbs. olive oil
6	Tbs. margarine
2	Tbs. fresh chopped parsley
	salt and granulated garlic to taste

◆ Start off by dipping chicken breasts in white flour. Add a little salt to the flour if you like. Saute breasts in olive oil until golden brown. Don't overcook.

◆ While breasts are cooling, in another pan add olive oil and margarine. Throw in sliced onions, sliced pepper and mushrooms. Saute until onions are translucent.

◆ Now slice chicken breast into strips and add to the onions and peppers.

◆ Add ½ of the almonds and ½ of the pecans. Throw in ½ of the chopped parsley and salt and garlic to taste.

◆ Toss the mixture together and place the whole mess in a casserole dish.

◆ Now place all the cheese over the top and sprinkle the rest of the nuts on top with some chopped parsley.

Eat hearty and remember me at Christmas!

Poki!

Meats & Poultry

MIRAMAR AT THE QUAY
216 Sarasota Quay, Sarasota

CHICKEN SACROMONTE
Serves 4

> 1½ lb. boneless, skinless chicken breasts
> 1 cup all purpose flour
> 1 cup bread crumbs
> 2 eggs, beaten with 4 oz. milk

◆ Coat chicken breasts on both sides with flour, dip in egg mixture and bread crumbs.

Sacromonte sauce;
> ½ cup margarine or butter
> 2 Tbs. fresh lemon juice
> 1½ cups beef broth
> 8 oz. smoked buffet ham, julienne

◆ Melt butter or margarine. When bubbling, add the fresh lemon juice. When this mixture starts bubbling again add the beef broth and mix well.

◆ Next add the strips of ham and let simmer for 5 minutes.

◆ Place a small amount of butter on a griddle (if griddle is not available use a frying pan), and grill or fry the chicken breasts until done.

◆ Place chicken breast on a plate and top with sauce. Garnish with grilled tomato and fresh parsley. Serve with rice or potatoes.

Better a sign which says No Entry
than one which says No Exit.
Anonymous

Meats & Poultry

Hyatt Sarasota
1000 Boulevard of the Arts On Sarasota Bay

Chicken Wrapped Around Asparagus
Chef Roger P. Michel

Ingredients are per 1 serving

6	oz. chicken breast remove bone and skin
	white pepper and salt to taste
8	medium asparagus
1	sprig basil leaves
½	cup chicken stock
1½	oz. Neufchatel (you'll find this in the dairy case)

For Pilaf:

1	Tbs. safflower oil
¼	oz. diced onion
½	cup chicken stock
½	oz. wheat berries*
2	Tbs cous cous
1	Tbs. parsley chopped

- ◆ Pound chicken breast. Peel asparagus and blanch until just crisp.
- ◆ Remove 4 asparagus and shock them with cold water. Cook remaining asparagus until soft.
- ◆ Season chickens with salt and white pepper.
- ◆ Place 4 asparagus in center and roll chicken breast firmly over asparagus, in sausage shape.
- ◆ Wrap chicken breast tightly with saran wrap.
- ◆ Poach 4-7 minutes in boiling water. Remove from heat.
- ◆ Reduce chicken stock by half and place stock and asparagus into blender or food processor. Puree until smooth. Return to pan, bring to a boil and stir in Neufchatel.

*A black or blue berry will do fine.

To assemble plate; spoon asparagus sauce on plate. Slice chicken breast into 4 rounds. Arrange over sauce. Serve with pilaf.

Pilaf; Saute onion in safflower oil Add chicken stock, bring to boil. Add cous cous until dry. Add wheat berries and chopped parsley. Adjust seasonings.

You can easily multiply this recipe to serve as many as you like.

MILANO'S
3589 Webber Street, Sarasota

POLLO ROLLATINI AMONTIA
Chef Bill Amontia

Serves 2

2-6 *oz. chicken breasts, boneless and pounded*
  6 *sundried tomatoes, chopped fine*
  1 *cup smoked Gouda cheese, shredded*
  1 *egg, beaten*
  1 *oz. portobello mushrooms, sauteed in butter*
  4 *scallions, chopped fine*
  ½ *oz. fresh basil chopped fine*
  2 *cloves **roasted** garlic*
  2 *pinches white pepper*
  2 *Tbs. prosciutto, chopped fine*

◆ In a mixing bowl, combine cheese and egg together. Fold in remaining ingredients and mix well.

◆ Chicken breast should be pounded evenly to an ⅛" thickness. Divide mixture between chicken breasts and spread out evenly. Roll and bake seam side down at 375° for 20 minutes.

While chicken is cooking make the sauce.

  4 *Tbs. pesto sauce*
  1 *red **roasted** pepper, sliced julienne*
  ¼ *cup heavy cream*
  2 *Tbs. Romano cheese, grated*

◆ Heat the heavy cream in sauce pan. Add cheese and pesto. Fold in roasted red pepper.

◆ When chicken is done remove from oven and let stand for 2 minutes. Cover serving plate with sauce. Slice rollatini and place around the plate. In the center, place fresh basil leaf for garnish.

Meats & Poultry

Piccolo Mondo Ristorante

3131 Clark Road, Sarasota

Pollo In Potacchio

Carlo Tonelli

Serves 4

3	lbs. chicken breast, boneless and skinless
¼	lb. butter
2	Tbs. olive oil
2	Tbs. black pepper
16	cloves garlic, leave whole
8	springs fresh rosemary
1	cup chicken broth
½	cup white wine

◆ In a large skillet, combine the butter, olive oil, black pepper, garlic cloves, rosemary and chicken broth.

◆ Set heat to medium high and add the chicken. Saute chicken for 4 minutes. Turn over and add the wine. Reduce heat and simmer until done.

◆ Serve chicken topped with sauce.

One father is more than a hundred school masters.
George Herbert

PASTA DEL GIORNO
2085 Siesta Drive, Sarasota

PASTA CON POLLO - *Pasta with Chicken*
Chef Angelo Cori

Serves 1

3	oz. fresh portobello mushroom or button mushroom, sliced
4	oz. fresh pasta
1	Tbs. sweet butter
3	oz. cooked chicken, diced
1	Tbs. marsala wine
2	oz. heavy cream
1	Tbs. grated parmigiano
	salt and pepper to taste

- ◆ Set a large pot of water to boil
- ◆ In a saucepan, melt butter and add the mushroom. Saute for a few seconds, then add the chicken, salt and pepper.
- ◆ Once the chicken has browned, add the marsala and turn up the flame until the alcohol has evaporated.
- ◆ At this point, start cooking the fresh pasta - remember it will take only a few minutes.
- ◆ Turn down the flame to the pan and add the cream and parmigiano.
- ◆ When the pasta is "al dente", drain thoroughly and add to the sauce.
- ◆ Combine well and serve with grated parmigiano.

◆ *Chapter Four* ◆

Fish & Seafood

Siesta Fish Market
Photo by Iris Rosenberg

SIESTA KEY FISH MARKET

Before there were any bridges to Siesta Key, Ida Blunt had a fish market there. For many years, local residents would pull their boats into the long winding canal on Siesta Key to buy and sell their fish and bait.

Later, bridges and roads connected Siesta Key to the growing population. Ida sold the fish market to Drum Wright.

About 1954, an enterprising young man Elvin Wilson bought the fish market. Elvin and Gloria raised their family around the fish market with everyone pitching in to help.

A sign was placed on Higel Avenue making the market easy to find. The sign still stands on Higel Avenue and has been designated as a historic landmark.

The original walls and ceilings still exist in the old market. Additions have been gradually made over the years.

Smoked mullet, oysters, sheepshead, croakers, drum, clams and blue crabs filled the counter in early days. Today you find shrimp, stone crab, pompano, grouper and delicious smoked mullet. Mullet is still smoked in the same smoke house built some 38 years ago. The roe of the mullet is very profitably sold to Japanese markets.

Marina Jack
2 Marina Plaza, Sarasota

Lemon, Dill, and Fennel Sauce
Chef Mary Moreno

Makes 1 quart

This is a very delicious sauce to serve with baked salmon, snapper, or chicken.

2	*pints heavy cream*
½	*stick butter*
1	*cup strong chicken stock*
	garlic, salt and white pepper to taste
½	*tsp. cracked black pepper*
½	*tsp. ground fennel*
1	*Tbs. dried dill weed*
	juice from 1 lemon or to taste

◆ Melt the butter on low heat, then add the chicken stock and all the spices.

◆ Bring the mixture to a simmer and add the cream.

◆ Cook on low for 5 minutes before adding the lemon juice.

◆ Bring again to a simmer and thicken slightly with a mixture of cornstarch and water.

THE FLYING BRIDGE
482 Blackburn Point Road, Osprey

MANGO AND SWEET PEPPER BUTTER
The Vroom family, owners

Makes 12 ounces

Whip 8 ounces sweet butter, fold in 6 ounces of mango, 2 ounces each of sweet pepper and yellow pepper, 1 ounce chopped scallion tops and 1 tsp. white pepper.

Roll in plastic wrap and chill.

Lightly season salmon with paprika. Pat salmon steaks with mango butter a few minutes before salmon is finished cooking

THE FLYING BRIDGE
482 Blackburn Point Road, Osprey

TOMATO SALSA WITH CILANTRO
The Vroom family, owners

Makes 16 ounces

10	ripe tomatoes peeled, seeded, and chopped
1	red onion, chopped
1	bunch green onions, chopped
½	bunch parsley, chopped
1	Tbs. cumin
1	Tbs. coriander
2	Tbs. cilantro, chopped
3	Tbs. wine vinegar
2	Tbs. sugar
1	Tbs. cayenne
	juice from one lemon
	juice from one lime
	salt to taste

◆ Mix all ingredients together, serve with grilled tuna or swordfish.

COASTERS
1500 Stickney Point Road, Sarasota

GRILLED MAKO SHARK WITH TEQUILA GINGER MARINADE
Chef Mark Kaiser

Serves 6

6	(6 oz.) Mako shark steaks, if unavailable Black-tip shark, tuna, or swordfish are excellent substitutes.
1	cup tequila
2	cups water
¼	cup Balsamic vinegar
½	cup grenadine syrup
¼	cup sugar
2	Tbs. fresh ginger, chopped
2	Tbs. fresh garlic, chopped
1	tsp. celery salt
1	Tbs. Kosher salt
	juice of 3 limes
1	cup virgin olive oil
1	cup hoisin sauce or substitute oyster soy sauce if you prefer
3	Tbs. cornstarch, diluted in water

◆ Mix the first 10 ingredients in a stainless steel bowl with a fine wire whisk. Slowly, add in the olive oil while stirring.

◆ For a finishing sauce, put aside in a sauce pan 1 cup of the marinade and add the hoisin sauce.

◆ Marinate the shark in a flat casserole pan in the refrigerator for 2 hours, turning every half an hour.

◆ Cook steaks on a hot charcoal grill for 8-10 minutes, or until cooked through. Baste steaks often with marinade while cooking.

◆ Bring to a boil the hoisin/marinade mixture. Add cornstarch mixture to tighten. Mirror the plate with the finishing sauce. Place Mako on the sauce and garnish with lime.

BANYAN
Ringling Museum of Art, Sarasota

GRILLED TUNA STEAKS WITH ROASTED RED BELL PEPPER AND BASIL SAUCE
Denis Cole

Serves 6

6	tuna steaks, 1" thick
¼	cup extra virgin olive oil
3	red bell peppers, roasted (procedure follows) and chopped
½	tsp. salt
¼	tsp. Tabasco sauce
½	tsp. white wine vinegar
4	Tbs. heavy cream
¼	cup fresh basil leaves, fine chop

To make sauce

In a food processor or blender, puree the roasted peppers. Add Tabasco, vinegar, and salt. Blend until smooth. Transfer the puree to a small saucepan, whisk in the cream and the fresh basil. Heat until warm but not boiling.

To roast peppers

Char peppers over an open flame for 4-5 minutes or until the skins are blackened. Transfer to a stainless steel bowl and cover with plastic wrap. Let cool until cool enough to handle. Peel and discard the seeds and ribs.

Cook the tuna steaks over a charcoal or gas grill for about 4 minutes per side. Baste with olive oil. Don't overcook the fish as it tends to become dry and tasteless.

Note: You may substitute swordfish or shark for the tuna. This bright sauce makes a stunning appearance.

PASTEL'S RESTAURANT
8920 Beneva Road, Sarasota

GRILLED HAWAIIAN TUNA WITH WATER CHESTNUTS, LIME, AND TOMATO SALSA
Chef David Shiplett

Serves 6

> 6 (7-8 oz.) tuna filets
>   Safflower oil, enough to coat fish

Teriyaki basting sauce:
> ½ cup soy sauce
> 3 Tbs. brown sugar
> 2 chopped green onions

Heat saucepan, add brown sugar, soy sauce, and onion. Let sugar melt then allow to cool.

Salsa recipe:
> 2 cups ripe tomato, diced small
> 1 cup Florida sweet onion, diced fine
> 1 oz. hot sauce
> 1 cup water chestnuts, chopped
> 2 Tbs. cilantro
>   juice of 1 lime

Combine all ingredients and chill.

To prepare fish:

Allow grill to get searing hot. Brush fish fillet with oil, don't over do it or your grill will flame up. The tuna will cook in 2-3 minutes on each side depending on the temperature of the grill and according to your taste. As it is finishing, brush the basting sauce on. Place fish on plate and sprinkle salsa on top to serve.

POSEIDON
3454 Gulf of Mexico Drive, Longboat Key

SALT COD BRAUDADE
Chef Christian Bousquet

Serves 4

3   lb. fillet of salt cod
2   cups virgin olive oil
3   cloves garlic, chopped
1   cup heavy cream
    white pepper

- ◆ Make your own garlic bread and cut up into croutons for later use.
- ◆ De-salt cod for 4 hours, changing water 4 times.
- ◆ Poach fish in low boiling water for 10 minutes.
- ◆ Remove bones and skin if necessary.
- ◆ In a skillet add 1 cup olive oil. When the oil is smoking, add cod and chopped garlic. Crush with a wooden spoon while heating gently.
- ◆ Remove from heat when it forms a paste.
- ◆ Gradually add ½ cup olive oil, a cup of heavy cream, and white pepper to taste.
- ◆ Transfer to an oven dish and brown at 350° for 15 minutes.
- ◆ Serve with garlic croutons around.

What the young one begs for, the grown-up throws away.
Russian Proverb

CAFÉ L'EUROPE
431 Harding Circle, Sarasota

DOVER SOLE PICASSO
August Mrozowski

Serves 4

> 2   whole dover sole (24-28 oz. each)
> 3   oranges, peeled
> 3   kiwis, peeled
> 6   large strawberries
> 2   bananas
> 6   oz. clarified butter or oil
>   lemon juice
>   white wine
>   flour and eggwash
>   salt and pepper

- Skin and fillet the dover soles. From the two dovers, you should yield 8 fillets.

- Heat a large skillet over hot to medium heat. Season and flour the dover, then dip in eggwash.

- Saute dover in a little butter, browning both sides until the dover is cooked completely - about 5-8 minutes. Before removing from pan, splash on some white wine and place dover on a heat tempered plate or tray.

- Cut fruit into ¼ inch slices, except strawberries which should only be cut in half. Arrange fruit in several rows on top of dover sole; oranges, kiwi, bananas, strawberries.

- Place plate under broiler or in stove until fruit is warmed.

- Cover fruit with drawn or clarified butter. Garnish plate with assorted vegetables.

The Colony Beach and Tennis Resort
1620 Gulf of Mexico Drive, Longboat Key

Chargrilled Scamp Florentine
Chef Jean-Pierre Pellet

Serves 4

2	*lbs. fillet of scamp or grouper skinless and boneless*
4	*bunches (handfuls) of fresh spinach*
2	*oz. no cholesterol margarine*
8	*asparagus*
3	*yellow squash*
4	*small tomatoes*

◆ Cut fillet into 7 oz. pieces. Heat grill ½ hour before cooking. Brush fillets with virgin olive oil.

◆ Cook fish on grill 7 minutes on each side. At the same time the fish is cooking, peel asparagus, and cut up squash. Steam both for about 3 minutes.

◆ Chargrill the tomatoes.

◆ Clean spinach and steam about 2 minutes.

◆ Cook spinach with margarine and a dash of lite salt.

Serve: put spinach in middle of plate. Place scamp on top. Arrange spinach around. Garnish with vegetables.

GECKOS
"At the Landings", 4870 S. Tamiami Trail, Sarasota

RED SNAPPER LIGHTLY BLACKENED WITH A RAISIN AND PECAN SAUCE
Steve Swenson

2 servings

Your favorite Cajun or Blackening seasoning. Figure one 5-7 oz. fillet of red snapper per person.

¼	cup olive oil
1	large shallot chopped fine
½	cup pecan halves
½	cup white raisins
½	cup chicken stock
4	Tbs. whole butter

◆ Lightly coat both sides of two 5-7 oz. fillet of snapper with blackened seasonings.

◆ Cook fillets in hot cast iron skillet until done. Set aside.

◆ In a separate skillet heat 2 oz. olive oil. Add 1 shallot, chopped fine, and 2 oz. pecan halves, and 2 oz. raisins (white if available). Cook for 1 minute and add ½ cup chicken stock. Reduce heat and slowly add 4 tablespoons whole butter stirring constantly until sauce thickens.

◆ Pour sauce over fish and serve with your favorite vegetable and rice.

Beach Cafe and Bar
431 Beach Road, Siesta Key

Poached Snapper
with Chardonnay Sauce
Manolo Cancho

Serves 6

1	qt. Court Bouillon
3	lb. Snapper fillets

◆ Bring Court Bouillon to a strong simmer in fish poacher or covered sauce pan. Place snapper in liquid and poach at gentle simmer for about 8 minutes or until fish is opaque all the way through.

Serve with Chardonnay sauce.

Chardonnay sauce:

2	cups Chardonnay
¼	cup shallots, minced
2	cups strong fish stock or clam juice
1	tsp. lemon juice
2	cups heavy cream
4	Tbs. butter
	salt and pepper to taste
	dash of Tabasco and lemon juice

◆ Boil chardonnay with shallots in sauce pan until wine is reduced to ¼ cup.

◆ Boil fish stock in separate sauce pan and reduce to 1 cup. Add chardonnay and shallot mixture. Stir in cream and gently boil until reduced to 1¼ cups.

◆ Turn heat to low and whisk in butter, 1 Tbs. at a time. Salt and pepper to taste. Stir in Tabasco and lemon juice.

OPHELIA'S
9105 Midnight Pass Road, Siesta Key

POMPANO IN PARCHMENT
Chuck Kelly, Jane Ferro, Stan Ferro , Proprietors

Serves 1, can easily be multiplied to serve more

7	oz. pompano fillet, center bone removed
4	cloves roasted garlic*
2	Tbs. salsa cruda**
1	tsp. sweet butter
1	Tbs. white wine
½	sheet parchment paper
	pinch of salt and pepper

◆ Lay pompano fillet in the middle of the parchment paper and top it with all the remaining ingredients. Fold paper in an air-tight fashion. Bake in 375° oven for 15 minutes.

* Roasted garlic - cut off top of garlic bulb, coat with olive oil and roast for 2 hours in 373° oven.

** Salsa Cruda - ripe (almost over-ripe), plum tomatoes marinated with olive oil, garlic, fresh basil, salt and pepper to taste.

Hyatt Sarasota
1000 Boulevard of the Arts, Sarasota

Mushroom Stuffed Grouper
Chef Roger P. Michel

Serves 1, can easily be multiplied to serve more.

5	oz. boneless grouper fillet
	dash of salt and white pepper
1	Tbs. lemon juice
2	shallots, minced
2	Tbs. olive oil
2	shitake mushrooms, sliced
1	large mushroom, sliced
1	slice tomato, peeled and sliced
½	cup clam juice or fish stock
3	large romaine lettuce leaves
1	tsp. chopped parsley
¼	cup dry white wine
½	cup clam juice or fish stock
¼	cup low fat sour cream

For garnish:

¼	tsp. cornstarch
1	tsp. salmon caviar
¼	cup jicama or boiled potatoes
	fresh seasonal vegetables, julienne

- ◆ Season grouper cutlet, (butterflied), with salt, lemon juice, and white pepper.
- ◆ Saute shallots in olive oil, add mushrooms. Add some fish or clam stock. Let reduce until dry.
- ◆ Add diced tomatoes and parsley. Let cool.
- ◆ Fill grouper with cooled mushroom mixture.
- ◆ Wrap blanched romaine or lettuce leaves around fish. Add fish stock and white wine. Poach for 3-4 minutes.

- ◆ Remove fish from poaching liquid and hold for service.
- ◆ Reduce fish stock. Add cornstarch dissolved with a few drops of water, cook until slightly thickened. Remove from heat and add low fat sour cream until smooth.

To assemble plate:

Spoon sauce onto plate. Arrange poached fish over sauce. Garnish with salmon caviar and serve with boiled potatoes or jicama and julienne vegetables.

TURTLES
8875 Midnight Pass Road, Siesta Key

BAKED FRESH SALMON ENCROUTE WITH ASPARAGUS BUERRE BLANC AND HOLLANDAISE
Eric Brown

Serves 6

6	(7 oz.) salmon fillets boneless and skinless
1½	lbs. fresh asparagus
¾	lb. sweet cream butter
6	(3"x6") sheets of puff pastry
	juice of 1 lemon
	salt and pepper to taste
	eggwash - 1 egg + 2 Tbs. water, beaten
	Hollandaise sauce

Rub salmon fillets with butter, lemon juice, salt, and white pepper. Place the 6 pieces of puff pastry on a clean, flat surface. Arrange salmon fillets on pastry sheets so that fillets are half in and half out. Brush edge of pastry with eggwash. Fold pastry around fillets and seal edges by pricking with a fork. Turn fillets over and place on a greased baking pan. Brush puff pastry with eggwash.

Nothing in life is to be feared. It is only to be understood.
Marie Curie

Sauce and garnish:

Wash the asparagus in cold running water. Trim the white part of the root off. This part is tough and not as sweet as the rest of the asparagus. Pick 18 nice spears out and coarsely chop the rest. Blanch all asparagus in boiling water until tender. Drain well and reserve the 18 spears for garnish. Puree chopped pieces in food processor until very smooth. Place in shallow saucepan and reduce over low heat, constantly stirring until mixture is thick (about 5 minutes). Remove from heat and let cool to the point just under hot. Swirl in ½ lb. of sweet butter with a whisk. Season with salt and pepper.

Bake salmon at 350° until done. Ladle Hollandaise in a circle on the top of plate (optional). Ladle asparagus buerre blanc in center. Place cooked fish on top of sauce and garnish by taking 3 asparagus spears and placing them between puff pastry and salmon, fanning them out. Serve immediately!

EUPHEMIA HAYE
5540 Gulf of Mexico Drive, Longboat Key

QUENELLES OF SALMON AND SCALLOPS WITH DILL
Ray Arpke

Serves 2-4

2	cups cubed salmon meat, remove all bones and skin
1	cup scallops
1	egg white
2	tsp. fish base (may substitute chicken cube)
½	cup Half and Half
1	dash white pepper
1	Tbs. fresh dill

◆ Blend together in food processor: salmon, scallops, egg white, fish base, dill, and pepper until smooth.

◆ Add the Half and Half through the fill tube while mixture is still processing. Process for a minute or two until you have a very smooth consistency. You may have to scrape the bowl a few times.

To Poach:

◆ In a large fry pan place enough water to reach 2" deep. Bring to a boil, then reduce heat to a slow boil.

◆ Salt the water to your taste. Take a tablespoon and scoop salmon mixture into boiling water in a rolling fashion, so as to make little eggs about 1" x 2".

◆ Carefully place them in the water. After they are cooked through, about 4 to 5 minutes, you may serve the quenelles on top of the sour cream dill sauce.

SOUR CREAM DILL SAUCE

 2 Tbs. chopped shallots
 ⅛ cup clarified butter
 ⅛ cup flour
 2 cups heavy cream
 1 Tbs. fish base
 1 dash cayenne pepper
 2 Tbs. chopped fresh dill
 ½ cup white wine
 ½ cup sour cream

◆ Saute shallots in butter for 1 minute.
◆ Add flour and cook 2 minutes longer.
◆ Add white wine, and cook 2 minutes longer.
◆ Add cream, fish base, and pepper, and cook 2 minutes longer.
◆ Turn mixture off, whisk in sour cream and dill. Serve at once or retain for later use.

Important: Do not let mixture boil when reheating.

What sunshine is to flowers, smiles are to humanity.
Joseph Addison

THE SUMMERHOUSE
6101 Midnight Pass Road, Siesta Key

BAKED SALMON ENCROUTE
Chef Paul Mattison

Serves 6

6	(6 oz.) fresh salmon fillets
12	sheets phyllo dough

Filling:

2	Tbs. olive oil
1	cup mushrooms, sliced
4	Tbs. chopped shallots
2	Tbs. chopped garlic
4	Tbs. port wine
4	Tbs. dry sherry
4	Tbs. lobster stock*
⅔	cup heavy cream
1	bunch fresh chopped basil
4	Tbs. cream cheese
	salt and pepper to taste

Sauce:

2	Tbs. olive oil
4	Tbs. shallots
2	Tbs. garlic
2	Tbs. brandy
⅔	cup lobster stock*
1	qt. cream
2	Tbs. dry sherry
	season with salt, pepper, and parsley

◆ **To make filling:** saute in 2 Tbs. olive oil the mushrooms, shallots, and garlic. Set burner on high. Ignite (deglaze) pan with port and sherry. Add lobster stock, cream, cream cheese, and basil. Reduce until sauce coats a wooden spoon.

For sauce:

◆ Heat saute pan on highest heat. Add olive oil and shallots. Deglaze (ignite) pan with brandy. Add lobster stock and reduce. Add cream and reduce again. Boil on high until you have desired consistency. Add sherry. Season with salt, pepper, and chopped parsley.

To assemble:

◆ Place a 6 oz. salmon fillet on 2 sheets of phyllo dough. Brush with butter. Add filling to top of salmon fillets. Fold in sides of phyllo and roll over 4 times, so the filling and sauce remain on top of the salmon. Brush with butter and bake at 350° until golden brown, about 15-20 minutes. Serve over sauce.

*Lobster stock

The day before:

◆ In a large pot cover lobster body with water. Add the next 5 ingredients. Bring stock to a boil, then lower heat and simmer 2½ hours. Strain stock through cheesecloth, cool and refridgerate.

lobster body

tomato paste

brandy or cognac

basil

carrot

garlic

It takes only a few minutes to put together the ingredients for the stock. You can do other things while sauce is simmering. Keep unused portion in refrigerator for 1 week for other uses or freeze in ice cube trays and save. You will be happy to have this wonderful stock on hand for future use!

L'AUBERGE DU BON VIVANT
7003 Gulf of Mexico Drive, Longboat Key

SALMON FILLETS WITH CHAMPAGNE SAUCE
Michel Zouhar and Francis Hatton

Serves 8

Start a day ahead, allow time for the sauce to reduce, and you'll find this recipe easier than you think. Stunning enough for the ritziest company.

For fish stock:
2   lbs. of salmon fillets and 1½ lbs. of heads, bones, and skin (your fish market should do this for you).
1   quart cold water
1   cup dry white wine
1   cup dry vermouth
1   carrot, coarsely chopped
1   med. onion, coarsely chopped
1   stalk celery, coarsely chopped
1   leek (white part), coarsely chopped
2   cloves garlic, crushed
2   bay leaves
    juice of 1 lemon
    generous pinch of tarragon
    generous pinch of thyme

To finish:
1   cup whipping cream
8   white mushrooms, sliced
3   shallots, minced
1   cup champagne
    pinch of cayenne

To prepare:

The day before:

◆ In a large pot, cover the fish head, bones, and skin with the cold water. Add the next 12 ingredients. Bring stock to a boil, skim well, then lower heat and simmer 2½ hours. Strain stock through cheesecloth, cool and refrigerate overnight.

To prepare fillets:

◆ Place fillets in a shallow, buttered baking dish. Top with sliced mushrooms and add just enough cold fish stock to cover. Cover and bake at 375° about 15 minutes, until just done. Remove and measure the liquid in which they cooked.

For sauce:

◆ In a heavy saucepan, saute the shallots in 1-2 Tbs. of butter until clear. Pour in the champagne. To the liquid reserved from the fillets, add enough of the remaining fish stock to bring to 3 cups. Add this to the saucepan, turn up the heat, and reduce the sauce by half (to 2 cups). Add the cream and reduce again by one third (to 2 cups). If you prefer a thicker sauce, prepare a roux of 2 Tbs. butter and 2 Tbs. flour. When sauce has reduced, taste for salt and pepper and add a pinch of cayenne. Leave as is or add enough roux to thicken to desired consistency.

To serve:

◆ Carefully lift salmon out of baking pan . Pour champagne sauce over fish to cover, include a few mushrooms and shallots on each piece of fish.

This recipe came to me courtesy of **Sarasota Magazine**, October 1991, by Mary Akashah.

THE SURFRIDER
6400 Midnight Pass Road, Siesta Key

SHRIMP BOMBAY
Javier Arana

Serves 4

28	large shrimp, peeled and deveined
1	tsp. shallots
¼	cup gin
1	tsp. soy sauce
1	tsp. ginger juice
1	Tbs. ginger root, chopped
1	cup scallions, chopped
2	Tbs. peanut oil
	salt and pepper to taste

◆ Saute the shrimp and shallots in olive oil. Add ginger root and juice and reduce sauce.

◆ Add salt and pepper and flambé with the gin. Add the soy sauce and let blend a few minutes.

◆ Before serving, add scallions and toss lightly.

No wife can endure a gambling husband,
unless he is a steady winner.
T.R. Dewar

MIRAMAR AT THE QUAY
216 Sarasota Quay, Sarasota

SHRIMP AND GARLIC

Serves 4

24	large shrimp, peeled and deveined
2	Tbs. ground garlic
½	cup olive oil
2	Tbs. white wine
	juice of 1 lemon

◆ Mix the shrimp with the garlic and set aside.

◆ Place oil in a frying pan at high heat. When hot, saute shrimp with garlic for 2 minutes moving shrimp so they will not stick.

◆ Add the white wine and let the liquid reduce, about 1 minute.

◆ Serve immediately and garnish with lemon and parsley.

HILLVIEW GRILL
1920 Hillview Street, Sarasota

LEMON SHRIMP
Mindy and Miles Millwee

Serves 4

12	oz. peeled and deveined shrimp (medium 40 count)
4	Tbs. oil (olive or canola oil)
	juice of 2 lemons
1	stick (8 Tbs.) butter
16	oz. fresh pasta - linguine or spaghetti

◆ Cook pasta
◆ Heat oil in large saucepan to medium high temperature. Add shrimp, saute quickly until ¾ cooked. Turn off heat, add lemon juice and butter. Add cooked and drained pasta to saucepan.
◆ Toss together, coating all pasta with liquid. Pull pasta from pan with tongs.
◆ Place pasta in bowl, pour remaining liquid and shrimp over pasta. Garnish with lemon slice and fresh parsley.

The Ca'd 'Zan,

Photo courtesy of John and Mable Ringling Museum of Art.

◆ *Chapter Five* ◆

Desserts

Mable Burton Ringling
Photo courtesy of John and Mable Ringling Mueum of Art

Mable Burton Ringling

 The Ca'd 'Zan, built in 1926 as the residence of John and Mable Ringling, was the epitome of locations for exquisite dining and entertaining.

Mable Ringling had a vision that became a reality with the completion of the Ca'd'Zan, which is Venetian for "House of John". Mable took a personal interest with every facet of construction, decoration, and furnishing of the estate.

The home was constructed of English veined marble, terra-cotta blocks, bricks, handmade Venetian tinted glass, red barrel tiles from Barcelona, and many other treasures collected from around the world.

Guests resided comfortably in the 30 rooms and 14 baths housed in the south wing. Eight thousand square feet of terrace, constructed in variegated marble, and enclosed by terra-cotta balustrades, welcomed friends.

The panoramic view of Sarasota Bay featured Mrs. Ringling's Venetian Gondola moored at the dock.

Unhappily, on June 1, 1929, only three years after completion of this historic home, Mabel died at the age of 54.

This historic landmark is open to the public. For further information call 351-1660.

BRIDGE TENDER INN

135 Bridge Street, Bradenton Beach

CHOCOLATE GODIVA PIE

Kathy Eubanks

Makes 1 pie

For filling:

12	oz. semi-sweet chocolate
5	oz. butter, unsalted
8	egg ~~whites~~ yolks
3	Tbs.. sugar
3	oz. whipping cream
¼	cup Godiva liqueur

- ◆ Melt chocolate and butter in top of double boiler.

- ◆ In a medium stainless steel bowl, beat egg yolks and sugar until light and lemon color.

- ◆ Add chocolate to egg mixture. Whip in heavy cream and Godiva liqueur. *together* Set aside.

Crust:

½	box Oreo Cookie crumbs
½	cup ground pecans
3	oz. melted butter

- ◆ Toss cookie crumbs, pecan, and butter together and press into 9" pie pan. Bake at 350° for 6 minutes. Crust does not have to be chilled.

- ◆ Add Godiva filling and refrigerate for 24 hours.

- ◆ Slice and top with whip cream and chocolate shavings.

Note: Kathy uses Belgian chocolate but, Hershey's will work.

Chez Sylvie
1526 Main Street, Sarasota

Chocolate Truffle Terrine
Sylvie Routier

Serves 6

>   12   oz. semi-sweet chocolate
> 1½   cups cream
>   ½   cup coffee liqueur
>   cocoa powder
>   6   hand picked strawberries
>   mint leaves

- ◆ Chop chocolate into small pieces.
- ◆ Bring cream to a boil, remove from heat. Add chocolate, stir using a whip until dissolved, add coffee liqueur.
- ◆ Pour into six ramekins. Refrigerate overnight.
- ◆ Sprinkle cocoa powder to cover each truffle and shake to distribute cocoa evenly.
- ◆ Garnish with strawberry and mint leaves.

BEACH BISTRO
6600 Gulf Dr., Holmes Beach

CHOCOLATE TRUFFLE TERRINE WITH MIXED BERRY MELBA
Chef Kathy Eubanks

Serves 20

27 oz. semisweet chocolate (Belgium or Hersheys can be used)
9 oz. butter

◆ Melt butter and chocolate in double boiler.

18 egg yolks
6 Tbs. sugar

◆ Whip yolks and sugar until light lemon in color.

¾ cup heavy whipping cream
3 Tbs. sour cream

◆ Whip cream and fold in sour cream.

◆ Add egg yolk mixture to chocolate and stir until yolk mixture is incorporated. Fold in whipped cream and pour in 9" spring form pan.

◆ Cover and refrigerate 24 hours. (Also freezes well.)

Mixed berry melba:
4 cups of either fresh or frozen berry mix, or, you can use just one kind of berry.
2 cups sugar

◆ Cover berries and sugar with water, (just enough to

cover berries). Bring mixture to a boil and reduce to one half volume.

◆ Run berries through food processor or blender and strain.

◆ Pour a puddle of berry mixture on bottom of chilled plate. Let terrine sit at room temp. for 10 minutes.

◆ Spring form pan will come right off.

◆ Slice chocolate and set in middle of sauce. Garnish with whipped cream and fresh berries.

This is a very rich dessert and a little goes a long way.

THE COLONY BEACH AND TENNIS RESORT

1620 Gulf of Mexico Drive, Longboat Key

CHOCOLATE PECAN TOFFEE MOUSSE
Chef Jean-Pierre Pellet

Makes 2 - 12" pies

The crust:
- 1   lb. pecan pieces
- 4   oz. unsalted butter
- ½   cup sugar
- 2   oz. water

◆ Grind pecans in food processor about 45 seconds and place in mixing bowl.

◆ Melt butter completely and add sugar. Keep heating and stirring until thick smooth paste. Remove from heat and add water stirring constantly to create a syrup. Pour mixture over pecans and mix thoroughly.

◆ Butter and flour 2 - 12" tart pans. Press pecan mixture into pans and place in 325° oven for 10 minutes or until golden brown. Remove and let cool at room temperature.

The Mousse:
- 28   oz. semi-sweet chocolate
- 32   oz. heavy whipping cream
- 2   oz. vegetable oil

◆ In a double boiler melt chocolate and add vegetable oil. Chocolate should be smooth and almost liquid.

◆ Whip cream to form soft peaks. Add hot chocolate while stirring constantly (slow speed of hand mixer will do fine). When chocolate and cream are combined, refrigerate for 2 hours.

◆ After 2 hours remove from refrigerator and stir by hand to make sure mousse is smooth and without lumps. Spoon into pastry bag and pipe mousse into pecan crust. Refrigerate complete pie.

The sauce:
Yields about 2 quarts
   1   *lb. unsalted butter*
3½   *cups sugar*
   1   *qt. heavy cream*

◆ Melt butter over medium high heat and add sugar. Stir mixture frequently. Continue this process until mixture has reached a deep caramel color. Butter and sugar at this point will be separating. No problem. Remove from heat and while stirring constantly, slowly add heavy cream. *Caution:* When adding the cream, mixture will bubble up and very hot steam will be released. I suggest using a whisk with a long handle or wearing an oven mitt.

◆ After cream is added, strain toffee sauce into container and let cool. Sauce is kept refrigerated and therefore will need to be heated when serving.

The best part!

To serve, cut pie into 12-16 slices. Serve individually with 2 oz. of toffee sauce ladled over.

When the fruit is scarcest it's taste is sweetest.
Irish Proverb

THE SUMMERHOUSE
6101 Midnight Pass Road, Siesta Key

CHOCOLATE MACADAMIA NUT TART
Chef Paul Mattison

Crust
Cream together:
- 1   cup butter
- ⅔   cup sugar
- ½   tsp. almond extract
- ½   tsp. vanilla extract
- 1   egg

Slowly add in:
2½   cups all purpose flour

◆ Chill dough 3 to 4 hours before rolling. Preheat oven to 350°. Roll dough to fit two 9" pie pans. Cut circle of wax paper and top pie dough with paper. Shake enough beans onto pie dough to cover bottom. This will prevent dough from bubbling up on the bottom. Discard beans when pie crust is done.

Caramel:
- ½   cup heavy cream
- 1½   cups sugar
- ¼   cup butter
- 1   cup Macadamia nuts

◆ Melt butter in small pan. Add sugar, stirring constantly until golden brown. Remove from heat and stir in cream. Cool slightly and add chopped nuts. Refrigerate caramel while preparing the chocolate cream filling.

Chocolate Cream Filling:
Scald in medium pan
  1   *cup Half and Half or cream*
  1   *cup sour cream*

Combine in mixer:
  2   *Tbs. cornstarch with*
  2   *beaten eggs*

◆ Beat together 2 egg yolks and 2 Tbs. sugar and add to
   the mixer.
◆ While mixer is going slowly, add the scalded cream and
   sour cream to the egg mixture.
◆ Return to saucepan and cook to a pudding consistency.

Stir in:
  6   *oz. semisweet chocolate,*
      chopped fine

◆ Pour caramel into baked empty pie shell. Spread
   chocolate mixture over chilled caramel layer. Refrigerate.
◆ Top with whipped cream, chocolate curls, and
   macadamia nuts as garnish.

To find a girl's faults,
praise her to her girlfriends.
Ben Franklin

CARAGUILOS
69 South Palm Avenue, In the Mira Mar, Sarasota

CHOCOLATE CHEESE CAKE

Serves 10

2	lb. softened cream cheese
¾	cup milk
1½	cup sugar
4	eggs
1	tsp. vanilla
1	pint sour cream
¼	cup flour
½	cup powdered cocoa

◆ Put all ingredients in mixing bowl, one item at a time. Blend until creamy.

◆ Pour into greased and floured 10" spring form pan.

◆ Bake at 325° for 1 hour, then turn off oven. Leave oven door open - allow to settle. Refrigerate 3 to 4 hours.

Pie crust is optional.

JACK'S CHOPHOUSE GRILL
Sarasota Quay, Sarasota

JACK'S CHOCOLATE BROWNIES
Pastry Chef Christian Dussualt

1	cup all-purpose flour
¾	cup granulated sugar
¼	cup brown sugar
½	stick butter
¼	cup shortening
½	cup brewed coffee
⅛	cup unsweetened cocoa powder
¼	cup buttermilk
1	large egg
½	tsp. baking soda (dissolved in a little buttermilk)
1	tsp. coffee liqueur

◆ In a large mixing bowl combine the flour and the sugars.

◆ In a heavy saucepan combine butter, shortening, coffee, and cocoa. Stir and bring to a boil on medium-high heat. Pour boiling mixture in the mixing bowl. Add the buttermilk, eggs, baking soda, and liqueur and mix well using a wooden spoon until well combined.

◆ Pour into a well greased 9" x 11" baking pan. Bake at 375° for 20 minutes. Remove from the oven and cool completely. Prepare the frosting.

Frosting:

9	oz. semi-sweet chocolate
1½	oz. butter
5	oz. milk
3	cups powdered sugar, sifted

◆ Melt the chocolate and the butter over a double boiler. Remove from heat and add the sugar and the milk. With a wire whisk, beat until smooth. Pour over cool brownies. Let cool and cut.

TURTLES
8875 Midnight Pass Road, Siesta Key

IRISH COFFEE CHEESE CAKE
Chef Eric Brown

6   whole eggs
3   lb. cream cheese
1   lb. brown sugar
3   cups coffee (reduced to ½ cup)
⅓   cup Kahlua
2   Tbs. vanilla
¼   cup Irish whiskey

◆ Cream eggs, brown sugar, reduced coffee, Kahlua, vanilla, and Irish whiskey until smooth. Add cream cheese and blend until smooth.

Crust:
◆ Line the bottom of a spring form baking pan evenly with 8 oz. Oreo Cookie crumbs (ground finely).
◆ Pack crumbs down tightly. Pour in cheese cake mixture.
◆ Bake at 300° for 1 hour and 15 minutes. Pull out of oven.
◆ Let cool to room temperature. Chill before serving.

Main Bar
1944 Main Street, Sarasota

Peanut Butter Pie
Family recipe

Serves 8

> *Whisk together:*
> ½ cup sugar
> 2 eggs
> 2 cups milk
> 2 Tbs. cornstarch

◆ Heat approx. 4 minutes in microwave, then whisk again.
◆ Heat for an additional 3 minutes then whisk again.
  Add:

> 1 Tbs. butter
> 1 Tbs. vanilla
> 1 cup peanut butter

◆ Mix well.
◆ Sprinkle 1-2 Tbs. grated coconut in bottom of graham cracker crust pie shell. Add batter.
◆ Top with peanuts. Serve with whipped topping.

That is an empty purse
that is full of other peoples money.
Anonymous

THE CHART HOUSE
201 Gulf of Mexico Drive, Longboat Key

CHART HOUSE MUD PIE
Dave Lynch

Serves 8

4-½	oz. chocolate wafers
¼	cup butter, melted
1	gallon coffee ice cream, soft
1½	cups fudge sauce
	diced almonds
	whipped cream

◆ Crush wafers and add butter. Mix well. Press into a 9"
pie plate. Cover with soft coffee ice cream. Top with cold
fudge sauce (it helps to put the fudge sauce in the freezer
for a while to make spreading easier). Store the Mud Pie
in the freezer for approximately 10 hours before serving.

◆ When ready to serve, slice the Mud Pie into eight
portions and serve on chilled dessert plates. Top with
whipped cream and diced almonds.

ALEXANDER'S RESTAURANT
At Kanes, 5252 South Tamiami Trail., Sarasota

BLACK BOTTOM BOURBON PECAN PIE
Paul Sauderman and Gary Magenta

Makes one pie
Crust:
3 cups flour
⅓ cup sugar
8 oz. butter
2 egg yolks

◆ Put flour and sugar in food processor and blend for
5 seconds.

◆ Cut the butter into pieces and add to the flour and sugar.
Blend for 15 seconds. Add egg yolks and blend until
dough forms into a ball.

◆ The crust can also be mixed by hand, cutting the butter
in with a pastry cutter. Roll dough into a 13" circle. Line
a 12" tart or cake pan with dough. Bake 10 minutes in
350° oven.

Filling:
6 eggs
2 cups sugar
4 Tbs. light Caro syrup
6 oz. semisweet chocolate
6 oz. butter
½ cup bourbon
10 oz. chopped pecans

◆ With mixer or food processor, beat eggs, sugar, and Caro
syrup until slightly thick.

◆ Melt chocolate with butter and bourbon in regular
saucepan.

◆ Beat chocolate mixture into egg, sugar, and syrup. Pour
into pie shell. Top with 10 oz. chopped pecans. Bake 35
minutes in 350° oven.

THE SURFRIDER
6400 Midnight Pass Road, Siesta Key

RUM CREAM PIE
Javier Arana

1 9" graham cracker pie crust
6 egg yolks
⅞ cup sugar
1 Tbs. gelatin
½ cup cold water
½ cup Jamaican rum
1 pint whipping cream
½ cup bittersweet chocolate, grated

◆ Beat egg yolks until light, then gradually add the sugar.

◆ Soak gelatin in the cold water. Place gelatin mixture over hot water, in top of a double boiler, and stir until the gelatin is dissolved.

◆ Pour gelatin over the egg and sugar mixture in a slow stream, beating constantly.

◆ Cool. Stir in rum.

◆ Whip the cream until very stiff and fold into the egg mixture.

◆ Cool the filling, but before it sets, pour into the pie shell.

◆ Refrigerate. When set, sprinkle with the grated chocolate.

Le Petit Jardin Cafe
218 West Tampa Ave., Venice

Lemon Walnut chess Pie
Gail Dempsey

Serves 8

1½	sticks butter
3	eggs
1½	cups sugar
⅓	cup fresh lemon juice
1	Tbs. flour
¾	cup chopped walnuts
1	9" unbaked reg. pastry crust

◆ Preheat oven to 375°

◆ Using a microwave, melt butter in medium mixing bowl. When butter bubbles up, remove from microwave and whisk in sugar.

◆ When sugar is incorporated, blend in eggs then lemon juice.

◆ Add flour and walnuts.

◆ Hand whisk until blended. Reduce oven temp. to 350°

◆ Bake approx. 45 minutes or until pie puffs up, nuts turn light brown, and filling feels firm when pressed lightly in the middle.

◆ For chocolate walnut pie: omit lemon juice and add ½ cup chocolate chips, 2 Tbs. cocoa powder, and 1 tsp. vanilla.

Serve pie warm with real whipped cream.

JUST DESSERTS
4783 Swift Road, Sarasota

FROZEN KEY LIME MOUSSE PIE
Susan Hoch

Serves 8

    6 *egg yolks*
    ¾ *cup sugar*
    ½ *cup Key lime juice**
    2 *cups heavy cream*
 9" *graham cracker crust*

- ◆ Combine yolks, sugar, and juice in double boiler over simmering water.
- ◆ Cook until thick (about 10 minutes), stirring constantly.
- ◆ Remove from heat. Cool to room temperature.
- ◆ Beat cream until stiff.
- ◆ Fold into yolk mixture.
- ◆ Pour into graham cracker crust. Freeze at least 4 hours before serving.

*Lemon juice can be substituted for lime juice.

BANYAN
John and Mable Ringling Museum of Art, Sarasota

FRESH TROPICAL MOUSSE
Denis Cole

Serves 6

½	cup fresh lemon juice
1	cup papaya or mango (pureed)
3	egg yolks
½	cup sugar
	pinch of salt
1½	Tbs. unflavored gelatin
½	cup cold milk
1	cup heavy cream (whipped)
2	Tbs. dark rum
1	pint strawberries, washed and hulled

◆ Add lemon juice to fruit puree.

◆ Beat egg yolks, sugar, and salt until thick and pale yellow in color. Add the fruit mixture and cook in the top part of a double boiler over water that is simmering (not boiling). Stir constantly until mixture thickens - do not over cook!

◆ Dissolve gelatin in cold milk and add to hot fruit mixture. Stir well.

◆ Chill mixture until it starts to set.

◆ Fold in whipped cream and rum.

◆ Place into serving dishes and chill until set. Garnish with fresh strawberries before serving.

TROPICAL FRUIT AND NUT TORTE
Chef Cheryl Wingate

Makes one torte

	pie dough for 2 crust 9" pie
¾	cup diced dried papaya
¼	cup amber rum
1½	cup sugar
1	cup water
1	cup heavy cream, room temp.
1¾	sticks unsalted butter, room temp.
⅓	cup honey
2	cups macadamia nuts, chopped

Glaze:

8	oz. semi-sweet chocolate chips
¾	stick unsalted butter
2	tsp. vegetable oil

◆ Combine papaya and rum, soak for 30 minutes.

◆ Cook sugar and water in heavy saucepan until sugar dissolves, swirling pan occasionally. Increase heat and boil until syrup is thick and caramel colored. Add cream, butter, and honey - stir until smooth. Return to heat, cook and stir 15 minutes.

◆ Roll ⅔ of dough to 9" cake or tart pan with a ½" overhang. Roll remaining dough to 9" circle.

◆ Fold nuts and undrained papaya into caramel mixture.

◆ Spoon into bottom shell and place pastry circle on top. Fold edges of bottom shell to seal. Cut a slit in top crust. Bake at 350° for 45 minutes.

- ◆ Prepare glaze over low heat or in microwave.
- ◆ Melt ¾ stick of butter.
- ◆ Add chips, heat and stir until chocolate has melted. Stir in vegetable oil.
- ◆ Cool until lukewarm. Let torte cool on rack 10 minutes. Invert onto serving plate and cool completely before glazing with chocolate

Happiness is a butterfly, which
when pursued, is always
beyond your grasp, but which,
if you sit down quietly, may
alight upon you.

Nathaniel Hawthorne

MICHAEL'S ON EAST
1212 East Avenue South, Sarasota

MACADAMIA NUT PEAR TART
Joey Jelenc, Pastry Chef

Serves 8-10

   1   cup sugar
   ½   cup light Karo
   ½   cup butter
   3   eggs, well beaten
   1   cup macadamia nuts, chopped
   ¼   tsp. allspice
   ¼   tsp. nutmeg
   3   ripe pears, sliced thin

Pastry Dough
   6   oz. macadamia nuts - finely chopped
   6   Tbs. butter
   ¾   cup flour
   ⅓   cup sugar
   2   Tbs. water

To prepare the tart shell:

◆   Mix well all pastry ingredients. Generously butter a 9½"
   tart pan. Press dough into pan and up sides. Bake at 350°
   for 8 to 10 minutes. After 5 minutes remove from oven,
   dough will have fallen from sides of pan. With the back
   of a spoon press dough up sides of pan and smooth out
   cracks on bottom, making sure tart shell is sealed.
   Return to oven and continue baking until light brown.
   After tart shell has cooled, place sliced pear pieces on
   bottom of shell slightly overlapping to produce a fan
   effect.

To finish tart:

◆ Mix sugar, Karo, syrup, and butter in a saucepan and bring to a boil. Cook for one minute.

◆ Remove from heat and stir to cool slightly. Slowly pour a small amount at a time of syrup mixture into eggs, beating continuously.

◆ Add nuts and spices then pour into prepared tart shell.

◆ Bake in a 350° oven for 45 minutes or until golden brown and bubbly. Enjoy!!

ROESSLER'S FLIGHT DECK
2033 Vamo Way, Sarasota

BANANAS FOSTER
Claus Roessler

Serves 4

> ½   cup brown sugar
> 4   Tbs. butter
> 4   ripe bananas, peeled and sliced lengthwise
> 1   tsp. cinnamon
> 2   oz. banana liqueur
> 4   oz. white rum
> 4   large scoops vanilla ice cream

◆ Melt brown sugar and butter in flat chafing dish.

◆ Add banana and saute until tender. Sprinkle with cinnamon.

◆ Pour in banana liqueur and rum over all and flame.

◆ Baste with warm liquid until flame burns out.

◆ Serve immediately over ice cream.

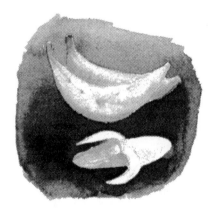

MILLIES
3900 Clark Road, Sarasota

LEMON SQUARES
From Millie

> 2 cups flour
> ½ cup powdered sugar
> 1 cup butter

◆ Mix together. Pat and press into a 9" x 13" pan. Bake at 350° for 20 minutes.

> 4 eggs beaten
> 2 cups granulated sugar
> ½ cup lemon juice
> ¼ cup flour
> ½ tsp. baking powder

◆ Pour into crust. Bake at 350° for 25 minutes. When cool, sprinkle generously with powdered sugar. Cut into squares.

AUGIE'S FRONT BURNER
3542 South Osprey Avenue, Sarasota

PEACH CRISP
Chef Augie Mrozowski

Serves 6

Peach Crisp:
10-12 fresh peaches sliced
- 1 Tbs. fresh squeezed lemon juice
- 2 Tbs. granulated sugar
- 1 Tbs. all purpose flour
- ½ tsp. ground cinnamon

Topping:
- ¾ cup packed light brown sugar
- ⅔ cup all purpose flour
- 6 Tbs. cold stick of butter (cut into small pieces)
- ¾ cup uncooked old fashion oats

◆ Pre-heat oven to 375° and have a 9" pie pan or 4-6" individual casseroles ready. Put sliced peaches in a large bowl, squeeze lemon over and toss.

◆ Mix together sugar, flour and cinnamon, sprinkle this over fruit and toss. Empty this mixture into your pie pan or individual dishes.

◆ To make topping in food processor, process brown sugar and flour to blend.

◆ Add butter and process with on/off turns until coarse crumbs form.

◆ Stir in oats with a fork. Sprinkle topping over fruit, then press down gently.

◆ Bake for 35-40 minutes or until lightly browned.

BRASS PARROT
55 Palm Avenue South, Sarasota

CARAMELIZED STRAWBERRY AND BANANA MERINGUES WITH CINNAMON-CHANTILLY CREAM

Makes 6 Meringues

> 3 egg whites
> 1 cup sugar
> 1 tsp. vanilla

◆ Let egg whites reach room temperature. Add vanilla and dash of salt. Beat to soft peaks. Slowly add sugar while continuing to beat, until very stiff peaks form. Cover sheet tray with parchment paper. Fit a pastry bag with a ½" wide round tip, and fill with meringue. Pipe out an oblong shaped nest about six inches long and three inches wide. Make six nests and bake at 275° for about 1 hour. Turn off heat and let dry in oven with door closed.

Prepare the filling:

◆ Take three pints fresh strawberries, wash and remove tops. Chop one pint coarsely and place in large skillet with ½ cup brown sugar and two tablespoons banana liqueur. Reduce over medium heat until mixture forms a thick syrup. Remove half the syrup and reserve. Place remaining strawberries and six bananas sliced lengthwise in skillet and toss gently with the hot syrup until coated well.

◆ Place two banana slices lengthwise in each meringue shell and fill centers with strawberries. Drizzle reserved syrup over top of each and finish with whipped cream spiked with a few drops of vanilla and a dash of cinnamon.

BEACH CAFE AND BAR
431 Beach Road, Siesta Key

THREE BERRIES IN LOVE
Manolo Cancho

Serves 6-8

½   cup Kirsch
½   cup sugar
5   cups of three berries, any combination
6   Tbs. butter, softened

◆   Combine Kirsch and sugar in a large skillet. Simmer gently over medium heat to form a light syrup and burn off the alcohol.

◆   Add berries and cook 3-4 minutes, shaking skillet to coat berries with syrup.

◆   Add butter and cook, still shaking skillet, until butter has melted.

◆   Stir gently so as not to break up the berries.

Serve warm with ice cream.

CHARLEY'S CRAB
St. Armands Circle, Sarasota

ORANGE CUSTARD
Chef Wesley Duval

3	eggs
1	egg yolk
⅔	cup of sugar
	juice of 3 lemons
	juice of 1 orange
5	oz. heavy cream

- ◆ Combine eggs, yolks, sugar and mix well. Add juices and cream. Pour mixture into a ceramic or glass ramekin. Bake at 300° for 25 minutes or until set. Chill.
- ◆ When ready to serve, run knife around custard and turn out into plate with raspberry puree.

Note:
Custard can also be baked in a tart pan with a cookie or short dough crust, provided you pre-bake crust before filling.

Winter comes fast on the lazy.
Irish Proverb

MILLIES
3900 Clark Road, Sarasota

OATMEAL COOKIES
From Millie

1	lb. butter or margarine
1½	cup brown sugar
1½	cup white sugar
4	eggs
1	Tbs. vanilla
3	cups flour
2	tsp. soda
2	tsp. salt
5	cups oatmeal
2	cups walnuts, chopped
2	cups raisins or chocolate chips

- ◆ In a bowl, mix together butter or margarine, brown sugar, white sugar, eggs, and vanilla.
- ◆ Sift in flour, soda, and salt. Add oatmeal, walnuts, and raisins or chocolate chips.
- ◆ Chill dough for several hours.
- ◆ Drop rounded tablespoons on greased cookie sheet. Bake at 350° to a golden brown.

"My favorite oatmeal cookies."

Photo: Rebecca Wild Baxter

◆ *Chapter Six* ◆

Restaurants Remembered

Gulf to Bay Club
Photo: Rebecca Wild Baxter

GULF TO BAY BEACH CLUB

It was called the Gulf to Bay Beach Club and its bartenders possessed the skill nearest akin to juggling: simultaneously keeping four blenders in continuous motion.

Just a short walk to the south of Siesta public beach, under the shade of the little thatched roof cabana, this bar's pina coladas withstood the toughest beach-goer's scutiny.

But it was more than just a drink formula.. The sand, the sun, and proximity to the water all made the "Gulf to Bay Beach Club" a perfect place to meet friends old and new.

This slice of heaven met the bulldozers only to be replaced by 300 condominiums. The new residents don't miss what they never new, but I will forever remember the "Gulf to Bay Club."

Perhaps you too have fond memories of special places where you have eaten, laughed and smiled. This chapter is about such places. It's about restaurants I remember.

The Field's Buccaneer Inn
595 Dream Island Road, Longboat Key

Chocolate Pecan Pie
Herbert P. Field

Makes 4 pies

8	squares baking chocolate
1	cup butter
3	cups white sugar
3	cups brown sugar
2	cups milk
1	cup karo syrup
4	tsp. vanilla extract
1	tsp. salt
12	eggs
	pecan pieces

◆ Over low heat - melt chocolate. Once melted, blend in other ingredients, stirring constantly until thickened. Pour into 4 10" pie shells, top with pecan pieces and bake at 300° until done.

It is much easier to be critical than to be correct.
Benjamin Disraeli

Restaurants Remembered

The Field's Buccaneer Inn
595 Dream Island Road, Longboat Key

Oysters Rockefeller
Herbert P. Field

6   oysters per person
1   qt. cooked spinach
1   lb. bacon (cooked crisp and chopped fine)
6   scallions
1   tsp. garlic
3   oz. pimentos
2   Tbs. Pernod
6   ozs. sour cream
1   tsp. black pepper
    Swiss cheese, grated

- ◆ Wash and trim spinach, steam for 4 minutes - set aside and drain well.
- ◆ In a saucepan with 4 tsp. clarified butter add scallions, garlic, pimentos, pepper.
- ◆ Saute for 3 minutes. Add Pernod.
- ◆ In a bowl, mix spinach with bacon and sour cream. Put 1 Tbs. on each oyster, top with Swiss cheese and bake in 300° oven for 8 to 10 minutes.

Note: During the proofing of this book, The Buccuneer Inn reopened for business under the new ownership of Tom Hires.

Restaurants Remembered

CASA AMIGOS
4994 South Tamiami Trail, Sarasota

ARROZ CON POLLO
(Sauteed chicken breast in light tomato and sour cream sauce)

Makes one very large entree

2	Tbs. butter or margarine
¼	cup dry sherry
1	tsp. chopped fresh garlic
10	oz. chicken breast cut in ½ cubes
¼	tsp. Worcestershire sauce
1	cup mushrooms (chopped in ¼'s)
2	Tbs. green onion chopped
½	tsp. black pepper
½	cup sour cream
1	Tbs. lemon juice
1	medium fresh tomato
10	oz. white rice cooked

◆ Make white rice, put to the side and keep warm.

◆ Gather all ingredients. Quarter mushrooms, chop onions, tomato. Put tomato into blender and puree. If making a large amount of Arroz you can use a canned crushed tomato if you prefer, approx. 5 oz. per serving. Saute chicken in hot skillet with olive oil, sear on all sides. Add garlic and sherry, lower to medium let simmer.

◆ When chicken is ⅔ cooked add sour cream, tomatoes, lemon juice, pepper and Worcestershire sauce. Using a rubber spatula combine well until you have a semi thick sauce. Turn heat to Add mushrooms, and green onions, simmer for 3 to 5 minutes.

◆ Place white rice on plate, using the bottom of a spoon, make ring by pushing rice toward the outer edge of the plate, (this create an edge that will prevent the sauce from running off plate). Place the chicken and sauce in the center of the plate. Garnish with a lemon wheel or wedge and sprinkle parsley top for added color.

COLEY'S
1355 Main Street, Sarasota

BANANA BAR
Chef Craig Soper

Sift together:
- 4 cups flour
- 4 tsp. baking powder
- ½ tsp. salt

Cream:
- 1 cup butter
- 1½ cups sugar

Add to creamed sugar:
- 1 tsp. cinnamon
- 2 tsp. vanilla
- 2 eggs, beaten
- 6 smashed very ripe bananas

◆ In a large bowl, stir together flour mixture and creamed sugar mixture. Slowly add ½ cup milk. Stir in 1 cup chopped walnuts. Bake in greased 12" or 13" cake pan, at 350° for 45 minutes to 1 hour.

◆ You may want to add chocolate chips or peanut butter chips or perhaps butterscotch chips to provide added sweetness and interest.

CLUB BANDSTAND
at the Sarasota Quay, US 41 and Fruitville Rd

CON QUESO

Serves 6

2   lbs. Velveeta cheese
½   onion - dice ½ inch pieces
1   tomato - dice ½ inch pieces
¼   cup diced fresh jalepenos
½   cup green chili salsa
7   oz. heavy cream

◆   Lightly saute onion, tomato, jalepenos, in 2 Tbs. vegetable oil.
◆   Add cream and green chili salsa and heat.
◆   Add cheese, constantly stirring until sauce is smooth and thick.

Serve with fresh corn tortilla chips.

Restaurants Remembered

CLUB BANDSTAND
at the Sarasota Quay, US 41 and Fruitville Rd.

BEEF FAJITAS

Serves 6

> 3 lbs. beef skirtsteak or chicken breast (boneless and skinless)

Fajita marinade:
For beef or chicken
- 2 cups vegetable oil
- ¼ cup red wine vinegar
- ½ cup chopped cilantro (loosely packed)
- ½ tsp. cumin
- 1 clove garlic, chopped
- ½ tsp. chili powder
- 1 tsp. salt

- ◆ Combine ingredients and mix well.
- ◆ Add meat, marinate overnight.
- ◆ Grill marinated meat to desired doneness. Slice into thin strips.
- ◆ Serve with flour tortillas, guacamole, sour cream, shredded lettuce, salsa and grated cheddar cheese.
- ◆ Serve buffet style and let each person make his or her own fajita.

Restaurants Remembered

MAAS BROTHERS
Washington Blvd. and Main Street, Sarasota

CHICKEN SALAD HAWAIIAN
Chef Ados Szabo

Serves 4-6

Line plate with leaf lettuce. Use leaf of head lettuce to form cup. Fill with ½ cup chopped lettuce and a little more than ½ cup Hawaiian mix (see below). Surround with fruit, such as:

5   orange slices (peeled and sectioned)
5   grapefruit slices (peeled and sectioned)
1   wedge of watermelon
    small bunch of grapes
1   wedge of cantaloupe

Top Hawaiian mix with pineapple ring and 1 tsp. *toasted* cashews. Comparable fruits in season can be substituted.

Hawaiian mix
1¼   lb. diced white and dark meat chicken
1   cup water chestnuts
1   cup celery
    dash of salt and pepper
1   cup Hawaiian dressing

Hawaiian dressing
Mix together:
2   cups mayonnaise
    dash onion salt
    dash ginger
    dash curry
½   tsp. soy sauce
2½   Tbs. wine vinegar
⅔   cup pineapple juice

Restaurants Remembered

MAAS BROTHERS
Washington Blvd. and Main St., Sarasota

FLORENTINE SALAD
Chef Akos Szabo

Serves 12

      2   *pkgs. lemon Jello*
      2   *cups hot water*
      2   *10 oz. pkgs. chopped spinach*
      2   *cups mayonnaise*
      2   *cups large curd cottage cheese*
      ½   *Tbs. vinegar*
      1   *cup chopped celery*
      2   *Tbs. chopped onions*

◆ Dissolve Jello in hot water. Chill.
◆ Just before Jello sets, mix in all remaining ingredients. Pour into 2" deep pan.
◆ Refrigerate until set.

Those who know they have enough are rich.
Chinese Proverb

MAAS BROTHERS
Washington and Main St., Downtown

BREAD PUDDING WITH RUM SAUCE
Chef Akos Szabo

18 Servings

1	lb. stale bread cut in ¾" cubes
6	eggs
6	cups milk
3	cups sugar
3	Tbs. vanilla
1½	cups raisins (soak in water, then drain)
4½	Tbs. butter, melted
1	tsp. cinnamon
½	tsp. nutmeg
1	cup chopped pecans

◆ Whip milk, butter, eggs until smooth and creamy. Whip in sugar then cinnamon, nutmeg and vanilla.

◆ Toss together bread, pecans, raisins. Grease two shallow 13" x 9" pans. Put bread mixture in. Pour milk mixture over. Let stand for 45 minutes. Flatten and bake 45 minutes at 350° or until firm.

Rum Sauce:

1	lb. butter
¼	cup milk
10	Tbs. cornstarch
4	cups sugar
4	egg yolks, beaten
½	cup rum

◆ Melt butter, stir in sugar, softly boil 7 or 8 minutes. Should be golden in color. Remove from heat. Whip in rum. Dilute cornstarch in ¼ cup of milk. Return to heat and whip until thickened. Remove from heat, let cool a bit, then *slowly* whip in beaten egg yolks. Serve on a dessert plate with a dollop of whipped cream as garnish.

Monique's Artist Palette Cafe
1377 Main St., Downtown Sarasota

Goat Cheese Salad
Monique Fisher

Truly not a boring salad! The Vinaigrette is classic.

◆ Mix several kinds of lettuce in a bowl with vinaigrette dressing, (recipe follows). Add some green pepper, garbanzo beans, olives (black and green), sliced onion and sliced cucumber.

◆ Toast white bread and cut in squares. Put one slice of goat cheese on each square and put under the broiler for about 1 minute - until warm but not melted. Arrange on top of salad bowl and serve.

Vinaigrette

6   Tbs. olive oil or ¼ cup + 2 Tbs.
2   Tbs. red wine vinegar
2   tsp. Dijon mustard
2   large cloves garlic
    salt and pepper

Mix well and pour over salad.

MONIQUE'S ARTIST PALETTE CAFE
1377 Main St., Downtown Sarasota

SHELLFISH BISQUE
Monique Fisher

Monique is well known for her soups and I think this is one of her best!

4	Tbs. olive oil
½	med. onion, chopped
2	Tbs. flour
6	cups clam juice
1	cup dry white wine
½	cup sherry
2	cups shrimp, chopped
8	mussels, chopped
1	cup crab meat
1½	cup clams, chopped
1	cup evaporated milk

◆ Cook onions in oil until transparent, add flour, mix well.

◆ Add clam juice a little at a time until well blended. Bring to a boil, add wine, sherry and all the seafood.

◆ Bring to a second boil and add the evaporated milk. Simmer and serve with Parmesan cheese and chopped green onions.

A little nonense now and then,
is relished by the wisest men.
Anonymous

Restaurants Remembered

OASIS RESTAURANT
3676 Webber Street, Sarasota

HONEY RAISIN GROUPER
Aldo Bagnara

Serves 4

Sauce:
◆ In a saucepan blend warm honey and red wine vinegar
at a ratio of 3 parts honey to 1 part red wine vinegar.
Add juice of fresh lemon to taste. I suggest juice of ½
fresh lemon per pint of sauce, which should be enough
for dinner for four.

Fish Preparation:
◆ I suggest you use fresh black grouper when available.
The black has a better texture and holds together better
than some grouper. I suggest six ounces per person cut
in two to three ounce fingers. Dip each finger in well
beaten egg and then dredge in flour. This can be done in
advance if you like.

Cooking:
◆ In a 12" saucepan bring a 50/50 blend of margarine and
100% olive oil to medium/medium-high heat. Brown
grouper fingers on one side. Flip grouper fingers and
add chopped Spanish onions (amount of onions is up to
you). Saute second side of grouper fingers until onions
turn transparent. Add equal amount of raisins and fill
pan approximately ⅓ inch full of sauce. On medium
high/high heat, heat sauce until it starts to foam. Turn
off or remove from heat if electric and cover. Let stand
about two to three minutes and serve.

OLD SOUTH OYSTER BAR
2215 South Tamiami Trail, Nokomis

MANHATTAN CLAM CHOWDER
Cindy Lakins

Makes 1½ gallons

1	can crushed tomatoes (16 oz. can)
2	cups **cooked** diced potatoes
4	cans chopped clams (6½ oz. cans)
2	bottles clam juice
1½	stalks celery cleaned and diced
2	large onions diced
1	lb. bacon cooked and diced

Seasoning:

1	Tbs. salt
3	shakes of Tabasco
1	oz. Worcestershire sauce
1	Tbs. white pepper

◆ Cook celery, onions, and bacon together until bacon is done.

◆ Add tomatoes and clam juice. Cook until celery is tender. Turn off heat and add clams and potatoes.

> You cannot do a kindness too
> soon, because you never know
> how soon it will be too late.
> *Anonymous*

PEPPERS BAR & GRILL
5864 Bee Ridge Road, Sarasota

GRILLED STEAKS
WITH BURGUNDY WINE SAUCE
Joseph Paquette

2 Servings

2   New York strip steaks

Prepare Burgundy wine and garlic sauce first by combining:

1   cup Burgundy wine
4   Tbs. chopped garlic
1   beef bouillon cube

Simmer 10 minutes. When reduced by half serve with steaks.

Baste steaks while grilling with mixture of:

1   cup Pat's Bar B Q Sauce
1   tsp. cracked black pepper
4   Tbs. Grey Poupon
4   Tbs. Catalina French dressing
2   Tbs. garlic salt

Restaurants Remembered

Robin & Joel's Restaurant
7500 South Tamiami Trail, Sarasota

Joel's Seafood Jambalaya

Serves 8-10

⅛ cup oil
1 Tbs. garlic
¼ cup soy sauce
¼ cup Worcestershire sauce
½ tsp. tabasco
1 cup ham or turkey, cubed
1 bunch celery, diced
2 large onion, diced

Seasonings:
¼ tsp. black pepper
½ tsp. salt
½ cup brown sugar

32 oz. crushed tomatoes
3 cups water
1 lb. shrimp peeled and deveined (raw)
½ lb. bay scallops
½ lb. blue crab meat claw, (picked, and cooked)
½ cup corn starch
1 cup water

◆ In a medium size pot add oil, garlic, soy sauce, Worcestershire sauce, ham or turkey. Add tabasco.

◆ Simmer for 3-4 min. Then add chopped celery, simmer and stir for 3 to 4 min. Add chopped onions stirring constantly.

◆ Add seasonings and continue stirring. Add crushed tomatoes and water. Bring back to boil. Add seafood. Stir well when boil comes back. Add corn starch and water solution to thicken. Serve over rice.

SHENKEL'S
3454 Gulf of Mexico Drive, Longboat Key

WELSH YORKSHIRE PUDDING
Edith Barr Dunn

Serves 4

     1½   cups flour
      ½   tsp. salt
      2   eggs, extra large
      ¾   cup milk, heated
      ¾   cup lukewarm water
     2½   Tbs. cooked beef drippings

◆ Preheat oven to 400°. Sift flour and salt together in bowl. Make a well in the center of mixture, put in eggs and pour in half of milk and half of the water. Mix well- then add remaining milk and water stirring until thoroughly combined. Cover with wax paper and set aside for 1 hour.

◆ Heat beef drippings in a small pan; pour (equal amounts) into small muffin tins then fill each half full with the batter. Cook in oven for 20 minutes.

Serve with roast beef or broiled beef.

Restaurants Remembered

Shenkel's
3454 Gulf of Mexico Drive, Longboat Key

Cattlemen's Veal Stew
Edith Barr Dunn

Serves 4

1¼	lb. veal leg or shoulder, boned and cubed
1	cup seasoned flour
2	Tbs. vegetable oil
3	shallots, chopped
½	cup dry white wine
¼	tsp. thyme
¼	lb. fresh mushrooms, sliced thick
¼	tsp. lemon juice
2	cups chicken stock, heated
1	Tbs. cornstarch
2	Tbs. cold water
3	Tbs. heavy cream
	dash of paprika
	salt and pepper

◆ Preheat oven to 350°. Cover veal cubes with flour. Heat oil in large, oven-proof casserole. When hot, put in veal cubes and sear for 7 to 8 minutes over medium heat. Turn cubes during searing to brown on all sides and season with salt and pepper to your taste.

◆ Add shallots, stir and continue cooking for 2 minutes.

◆ Pour in wine, add thyme, mix and cook for 2 minutes over heat raised to high. Reduce heat to medium, add mushrooms and lemon juice.Cook an additional 2 minutes.

- Pour in heated chicken stock, adjust seasoning if necessary and bring to a boil. Mix cornstarch with water and stir into the stew as it approaches boiling. Reduce heat to medium and cook for 1 minute to thicken somewhat.

- Stir in cream, put in paprika, make final seasoning adjustments if you desire. Cover casserole and cook in the preheated oven for 1½ hours.

- Serve with a vegetable side dish.

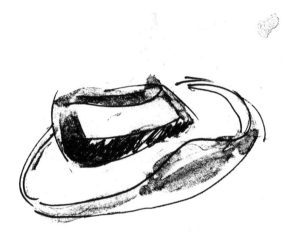

STICKNEY POINT FISHERY
1266 Old Stickney Point Rd., Siesta Key

SHRIMP CREOLE

Serves 4

1	large onion - chopped med. pieces
1	large green pepper - chopped medium
2	large stalks celery - chopped larger
¼	cup olive oil
4	medium large tomatoes - peeled and chopped
2	cups Knorrs fish bouillon
	pinch of cayenne
2	bay leaves
1	tsp. basil
1	tsp. Worcestershire sauce
2	lb. large shrimp, peeled and deveined

◆ In large pot, saute onion, pepper and celery in oil for 5 minutes.

◆ Add tomatoes, fish stock, cayenne, bay leaf, basil and simmer on low for 45 minutes.

◆ Add shrimp and continue simmering for about 10 minutes.

◆ This can be served over white rice.

Note: During the proofing of this book, the "Stickney Point Fishery" has reopened with Chef Eric Brown.
This recipe is from the original Stickney Point Fishery and is not Chef Eric's.

TASSOTTI'S
7321 S. Tamiami Trail, Sarasota

FETTUCCINE ALFREDO
Giocondo Tassotti

Serves 4

1	lb. fresh egg fettuccine
1½	pt. heavy cream
½	lb. Parmesan cheese (reggiano)
4	Tbs. butter
3	egg yolks

◆ Heat cream and butter until boiling.

◆ Add cooked fettuccine. Bring back to boil.

◆ Add egg yolks, and Parmesan cheese, stirring continuously.

◆ Bring to boil, remove from heat and serve with fresh ground pepper.

He who limps is still walking.
Swiss Proverb

TASSOTTI'S
7321 S. Tamiami Trail, Sarasota

SCAMPI AL BURRO
Giocondo Tassotti

Serves 4

24	large shrimp
4	cloves fresh garlic (chopped)
2	sprigs parsley (chopped)
1	cup butter
½	lb. angel hair pasta

◆ Melt butter in a saute pan.

◆ Add garlic and shrimp to butter and cook for 10 minutes.

◆ Remove shrimp from pan and put aside. Add cooked angel hair pasta to saute pan. Add parsley, salt and pepper to taste. Mix and serve with shrimp on top.

Restaurants Remembered

VITO'S
3589 Webber Street, Sarasota

ESPRESSO CHEESE CAKE
Thomas Dinsmore

Crust:
1½   cups hazelnuts
⅓   cup sugar
3   Tbs. melted butter
1   Tbs. coca powder

◆   Mix all together, press into bottom of a 10" springform pan. Bake 10 minutes at 325°. Cool and wrap bottom and sides with aluminum foil.

Filling:
1   cup liquid espresso
24   oz. cream cheese
1⅓   cup sugar
1½   Tbs. cornstarch
¼   tsp. salt
1½   tsp. lemon peel
3   large eggs (room temperature)
3   large egg yolks (room temperature)
⅓   cup Half and Half
¼   cup lemon juice
1   Tbs. coffee liqueur
½   tsp. vanilla extract

◆   Simmer espresso to reduce volume to ¼ cup. cool. Mix cream cheese, sugar, cornstarch, and salt, until smooth. Beat in eggs and yolks one at a time. Mix in remaining ingredients and let stand 15 minutes, pop air bubbles with a toothpick. Pour into pan with crust. Place into large roaster with water, (water should come half way up the sides of springform pan.) Bake at 325° for 1½ hours.

WHISPER INN
8197 South Tamiami Trail, Sarasota

CHICKEN ANNO
House Recipe

Serves 4

4 chicken breasts, skinless and boneless
  melted butter
  garlic
  paprika
8 slices bacon
2 cups thick cream sauce
  salt and pepper to taste
1 cup grated Cheddar cheese
3 Tbs. sherry
1 cup cooked chopped spinach (optional)
  Parmesan cheese

◆ Fold bacon around chicken breasts. Place breasts in a pan. Brush with garlic butter and season with paprika. Place in a preheated, 400° oven. Cook until done.

◆ Meanwhile, prepare your favorite cream sauce. Season to taste with salt and pepper. Blend in Cheddar cheese, sherry and spinach.

◆ Place cooked breasts with bacon in a casserole dish. Pour sauce over chicken. Sprinkle with Parmesan cheese. Brown under broiler and serve.

The girl who can't dance says the band can't play.

Yiddish Proverb

Index

Index

◆185◆

Index

Index

Index

Index

Index

Index

FISH ARITHMETIC

Shrimp in one pound

Size	No. of raw shrimp in shell from 1 pound
Jumbo	12 to 15
Large	15 to 18
Medium	26 to 30
Tiny	50 or more

How much to serve for one average entree serving

Shrimp
shelled	¼ lb.
in shells	6 jumbo or 8 large

Crab
whole, blue	2 to 4
whole, Dungeness	1
Crab meat	¼ lb.

Lobster
whole	1 lb.
tail	½ lb.
meat	¼ lb.

Stone Crab Claws
large	1¼ lb.

Clam
shucked	¾ cup
in shells as appetizer	6
in shells as entree	12

Oysters
shucked	¾ cup
in shells as appetizer	6
in shells as entrees	16 to 20

Fish
whole	12 oz.
fillets or steaks	¼ lb.

Index

TARRAGON   SAGE   MINT   THYME   PARSLEY   BASIL

DILL

ROSEMARY

CHIVES

SAGE

THYME

PARSLEY

MINT

GARLIC

Index

Index by Restaurant

Index

Index

Photo: Rebecca Wild Baxter

Index

ORDER FORM
Sarasota's Chef Du Jour

3712 Woodmont Drive
Sarasota, Florida 34232

Please send _____ copy (ies) of
Sarasota's Chef Du Jour to:

Name _____

Address: _____

City: _____

State: _____

Quantity: _____ at $13.00   = _____

Postage and Handling $3.00 per book   = _____

TOTAL ENCLOSED: = _____
  (Check or Money Order)